I0450642

10 Powerful
TAX STRATEGIES
That Pass IRS Scrutiny

10 POWERFUL
TAX STRATEGIES
THAT PASS IRS SCRUTINY

▼

Reduce Your Taxes Beginning Today!

Brent J. Jordan

Attorney at Law
Master of Laws in Taxation

Writers Club Press
San Jose New York Lincoln Shanghai

10 Powerful
TAX STRATEGIES
That Pass IRS Scrutiny

All Rights Reserved © 2002 by Brent J. Jordan

No part of this book may be reproduced or transmitted in any form or by any means, graphic, electronic, or mechanical, including photocopying, recording, taping, or by any information storage retrieval system, without the permission in writing from the publisher.

Writers Club Press
an imprint of iUniverse, Inc.

For information address:
iUniverse, Inc.
5220 S. 16th St., Suite 200
Lincoln, NE 68512
www.iuniverse.com

Warning—Disclaimer

This book contains the author's opinions in regard to the subject matter of eliminating taxes. The author made every effort to provide accurate, up-to-date, and authoritative information regarding the subject matter covered herein. There may, however, be some errors of subject matter. The author makes no guarantees, warranties, or representations of any kind. This book is sold and read with the understanding that the author is not engaged in rendering professional or legal advise or services of any kind.

ISBN: 0-595-21281-6

Printed in the United States of America

This book is dedicated to my wife Kathy
whose ten fingers changed Connor and Noah's diapers
while mine danced upon a computer keyboard
to change our view of taxes.

CONTENTS

CHAPTER ONE

▼

REDUCE YOUR TAXES BEGINNING TODAY!

Do you have a current tax plan? If you smile and proudly answer "yes," then congratulations! You're one of a very select group of Americans. In fact, you probably acquired this book to make certain your tax plan did not leave any stone unturned.

But if you're like most Americans, when confronted with this basic question, you're more likely to shrug your shoulders with a puzzled look on your face, then shake your head "no." If this sounds like you, I want you to remember one very important point: If you do not have a current tax plan, you still have a plan. You've simply planned to pay more than your fair share of taxes to Uncle Sam.

Now the purpose of my question is not to praise or criticize you, but to awaken your passion, to make you realize that a few simple tax strategies can put more money in your pocket year after year after year. I'm not just talking about saving a few tax dollars, but slashing your taxes to the bare bone, if not actually eliminating them altogether from your life.

Is that actually possible? Is it legal? You're about to find out. So let me take you to the promise land. Without wasting one more single word, let's go straight for the juggler vein. I call it "The Holy Grail."

The Holy Grail

Any tax reduction strategy can be reduced to three powerful principals.

You must maximize:

(1) Tax-free, Tax-reduced, and Tax-deferred income;

(2) Adjustments, Deductions, Exemptions, & Credits;

(3) Shifting of taxable income and deductions to future and current tax years, and other taxpayers.

United States Federal Justice Learned Hand once wrote: "Anyone may so arrange his affairs that his taxes shall be as low as possible; he is not bound to choose that pattern which will best pay the Treasury; there is not even a patriotic duty to increase one's taxes." 69 Fed.2d 809,810

So there you have it. Ten tax strategies contained within three powerful principals and, best of all, a big kiss of approval from our United States court system. And that's why the IRS fears me. Because I'm going to show you just how easy it is to reduce, even possibly eliminate, your taxes.

What I'm Not Going To Do

Before I tell you what I'm going to do about slashing your taxes, let me first tell you what I'm not going to do in this book.

I'm not going to overwhelm you with a scholarly treatise on the Internal Revenue Code. The same Justice Learned Hand once wrote: "The words of such an act as the [Internal Revenue Code] merely dance before my eyes in a meaningless procession: cross-reference, exception upon exception—couched in abstract terms that offer no handle to seize hold of—leave in my mind only a confused sense of some vitally important, but successfully concealed, purport, which it is my duty to extract, but which is within my power, if at all, only after the most inordinate expenditure of time. I know that these monsters are the result of fabulous industry and ingenuity, plugging up this hole and casting out the net, against all possible evasion; yet at times I cannot help recalling a saying of William James about certain passages of Hegel: that they were, no doubt, written with a passion of rationality; but that one cannot help wondering whether to the reader they have any significance save that the words are strung together with syntactical correctness..." 57 Yale L.J. 167, 169 [1947]

I'm also not going to waste your time with an academic discourse on the legal and social theories of taxation. When asked whether he understood the United States Tax Code, Albert Einstein simply replied: "I am a mathematician, not a philosopher."

And I'm not going to bore you with a detailed history of the United States tax system. A newspaper reporter once said: "When men get in the habit of helping themselves to the property of others, they cannot easily be cured of it. The history of our tax code, in economic terms, mirrors the course of most addictions; advancing dependence, diminishing returns, and deteriorating health of the afflicted." 1909 Newspaper Editorial Opposing the Very First Income Tax

Instead, I'm going to serve you meat and potatoes. I'm going to provide concrete strategies that will eliminate or substantially reduce your taxes beginning today. So let's stop with the introduction and start with the learning, beginning with how the IRS calculates your tax liability.

Calculating Your Taxes

If you asked an IRS agent how to calculate your taxes, the agent might explain the process like this:

When preparing a tax return, once you've determined your "gross income," subtract certain adjustments from gross income to arrive at your "adjusted gross income." Next, subtract deductions and exemptions from adjusted gross income to arrive at your "taxable income." Next, apply the "tax tables" to your taxable income to calculate your "tax liability." Finally, subtract "tax credits" from your tax liability to arrive at your "actual tax" which is the tax you pay the IRS.

If I incorporate this monologue into a single chart, here is what it would look like:

Gross income – Adjustments (above the line deductions)
= Adjusted Gross Income.

Adjusted Gross Income – below the line deductions &
Exemptions = Taxable Income.

Tax Tables applied to Taxable Income = Tax Liability.

Tax Liability – Tax Credits = Actual Tax payment to IRS.

If all these terms and calculations seem foreign and a bit confusing, don't worry about it. Tax terminology humbles the most brilliant minds.

Let's begin with "gross income." In the next section, I will define this term in great detail. For the moment, simply think of gross income as work-related earnings and investment income, or what I like to refer to as ordinary taxable income. It does not include tax-free income: income the IRS does not tax. It does not include tax-deferred income: income the IRS taxes in a future year. It does include tax-reduced income: income the IRS taxes, but at a preferred tax rate. You do not calculate your taxes based upon gross income.

Instead, our federal government permits you to subtract certain expenses, otherwise known as adjustments, from gross income to arrive at a lower income figure called adjusted gross income. You do not calculate your taxes based upon adjusted gross income.

Instead, our federal government permits you to subtract even more expenses, otherwise known as deductions, along with a certain dollar amount based upon your marital status and household dependents, otherwise known as exemptions, to arrive at an even lower income figure called taxable income. You do calculate your tax liability based upon taxable income, but you do not pay this amount to the IRS.

Instead, the federal government permits you to subtract a certain dollar amount based upon your economic status and social activities, otherwise known as credits, to arrive at your actual tax. You do pay this amount to the IRS.

Now let's turn our attention to public tax enemy number one: Gross Income! Or what I like to refer to as ordinary taxable income.

Ordinary Taxable Income

To reduce taxes, you must first learn about gross income, or what I call ordinary taxable income.

Internal Revenue Code section 61 defines gross income as: "Except as otherwise provided in this subtitle, gross income means all income from whatever source derived, including compensation for services, including fees, commissions, fringe benefits, and similar items; gross income derived from business; gains derived from dealings in property; interest; rents; royalties; dividends; alimony and separate maintenance payments; annuities; income from life insurance and endowment contracts; pensions; income from discharge of indebtedness; distributive share of partnership gross income; income in respect of a decedent; and income from an interest in an estate or trust."

But you did not acquire this book to learn what constitutes gross income? You want to learn what does <u>not</u> constitute gross income?

The answer lies in the opening phrase of section 61: "Except as otherwise provided in this subtitle,..." And that's what Chapter One is all about: the word "except." You need to identify all the exceptions to gross income. You need to learn how to convert gross income, or what I refer to as ordinary taxable income, into tax-free income or, if that's not possible, convert ordinary taxable income into tax-reduced income or, if that's not possible, convert ordinary taxable income into tax-deferred income. You get three bites of the apple.

As you have just seen, gross income, or what I refer to as ordinary taxable income, includes wages, salaries, and tips, along with commissions, self-employment income, interest, dividends, rents, royalties, and alimony. In a nutshell, ordinary taxable income usually involves work-related earnings.

If you remember only one lesson about ordinary taxable income, remember this: it should be avoided like the plague. Why? Because the IRS taxes this income at the highest possible rate. In some cases, the IRS confiscates more than 50% of your earnings. Is that really possible? Not only is it possible, it's 100% certain, unless you implement a carefully designed tax plan.

Before we create this tax plan, I want you to understand a few important points. First the good news. If your annual earnings do not exceed a specific dollar amount, you pay zero taxes that year. Nor will the IRS carry-over your earnings to the next year. You start fresh each year.

More good news. Even if your annual earnings do exceed a specific dollar amount, and thus require you to pay taxes, you will not pay the same tax rate on all your earnings. The U.S. has a "progressive" tax rate system. The IRS taxes your earnings at different tax rates that progress upward as your income progresses upward. Whether your rich or poor or middle class, everyone pays the same tax rate on the first thousand dollars of income. This equality continues until one's income reaches the maximum tax rate, at which point the progressive tax rate system comes to an abrupt end, and everyone pays the same rate on an unlimited amount of earnings.

Now for the bad news. If your annual earnings require you to pay taxes, you will pay not just one, but three separate taxes. From your paycheck, the IRS first seizes income taxes. But that's not good enough. The IRS then grabs two additional taxes: FICA (Medicare and Social Security taxes) and FUTA (Federal Unemployment taxes).

"Wait a second," you might say. "I only pay half of those FICA and FUTA taxes. My employer pays the other half." Wrong. Wouldn't you're employer rather pay you this half instead of the IRS? Of course. So that's how our government can potentially seize more than half your earnings: income taxes plus FICA taxes plus FUTA taxes equal more money for the IRS and less money for you.

By now you must realize why ordinary taxable income seems like a four letter word, something to avoided whenever possible. Don't fool yourself. If you decide not to implement a carefully designed tax plan, you still have a plan. You've planned to accept the IRS plan. Whose financial interest do you think they're looking out for? Alright then, let's start learning the ten tax strategies.

CHAPTER TWO

▼

REDUCE TAXABLE INCOME

This chapter focuses primarily upon "income." You will learn how to convert gross income, or what I refer to as ordinary taxable income, into a special kind of income. This special kind of income will be subject to one of three tax treatments: zero taxes, substantially reduced taxes, or deferred taxes.

In the next chapter, we will focus our attention primarily upon "expenses." You will learn how to reduce gross income by means of special kinds of expenses given favorable treatment by Congress. These expenses concern four tax concepts: adjustments, deductions, exemptions, and credits.

In the final chapter on tax strategies, we will focus our attention primarily upon "tax shifting." You will learn how to shift income and expenses to the most beneficial tax year and taxpayer.

So let's get started without any further delay, beginning with the grand-daddy of all tax strategies: converting taxable income to tax-free income.

TAX STRATEGY #1

Tax-Free Income

Tax-free income is just what it sounds like, income for which you pay zero taxes. Unlike ordinary taxable income, tax-free income should be pursued whenever possible. The IRS cannot seize one penny of this very special category of income.

Congress intended certain income to escape taxation in order to implement economic and social goals. Don't argue with Congress. Pursuing tax-free income is perfectly legal, and perfectly smart. Are you ready to learn more than fifty tax-free strategies? I thought so.

Home

Home Sale: You pay zero taxes on the sale or exchange of your home if you owned and occupied it as your principal residence for at least two out of the past five years, and your gain did not exceed $250,000 for a single person or $500,000 for a married couple. The definition of "home" includes a mobile home, trailer, houseboat, townhouse, and condominium.

Vacation Home: You pay zero taxes on income received as a result of renting your vacation home during any given year, provided you limit such rental to the lesser of 14 days or 10% of the fair market rental days.

"Like-Kind" Exchange: You pay zero taxes when you exchange business or investment property for similar property, provided: (1) each property has the same tax identity and fair market value; (2) you designate the new property within 45 days of the exchange; and (3) you complete the exchange within 180 days.

Family

Gifts Received: You pay zero "current" taxes on any gift you receive from another person, regardless of value or quantity, and whether such gift involves cash, securities, real or personal property. However, if you later sell this gift, you owe taxes on the difference between the sale price and the price paid by the individual who gave it to you. Any gift in excess of a limited amount may also cause the individual who gave you the gift to pay a gift tax.

Family Limited Partnership: You pay zero taxes for certain income earned by your family investment account. Here is how it works. First, you create a Family Limited Partnership or Limited Liability Company, and designate yourself as the general partner or manager and the limited partner or member. Second, you place investment assets into this investment entity. Third, you invest and spend the assets as you alone decide. Finally, each year, in exchange for services or simply as tax-free gifts, you assign limited partnership interests to family members in lower tax brackets.

This strategy allows you to retain 100% control of the partnership assets and, at the same time, shift all tax liability to your limited partners.

Children's Earned Income: Your children, grand-children, parents, grand-parents, nieces, nephews, and other family relatives pay zero taxes on a limited amount of earnings they receive each year as employees of your family business.

<u>**Children's Unearned Investment Income**</u>: Your children, grandchildren, parents, grandparents, nieces, nephews, and other family relatives pay zero taxes on a limited amount of investment income they receive each year.

<u>**Charitable Remainder Trust**</u>: You pay zero taxes on income resulting from the appreciation of your assets. To obtain this tax-free income, you must first transfer appreciated assets to an IRS approved charity or family foundation. By doing so, you will receive an enhanced stream of income for life, a tax deduction based upon the value of your transferred assets, and tax-free appreciation of the assets. As an extra bonus, you also remove these assets from your estate and thus eliminate estate taxes.

<u>**Damage Awards**</u>: You pay zero taxes for money received as a result of a personal injury claim involving physical injury or sickness, or as a result of a property damage claim.

<u>**Divorce Settlements**</u>: You pay zero taxes for child support payments received from your spouse, as well as money received as a result of a marital property settlement or family court judgment.

<u>**Public Assistance Payments**</u>: You pay zero taxes for money you receive from a general welfare fund, such as payments to aid the indigent, blind persons, and crime victims.

<u>**Awards and Prizes**</u>: You pay zero taxes for any award or prize you receive in recognition of a past accomplishment, but only if you assign the award or prize to a governmental unit or charitable organization.

Work

Tax-Free State Income: You pay zero state taxes for any income you receive as a resident of Nevada, Florida, Alaska, South Dakota, Wyoming, and Washington. You pay zero state taxes for earned income you receive as a resident of New Hampshire and Tennessee, but these states require you to pay taxes for unearned interest and dividend income.

Foreign Income: As a U.S. citizen, you pay zero U.S. taxes on a limited amount of annual wages and salaries earned in a foreign country, provided you reside in a foreign country during the full tax year or are physically present in a foreign country at least 330 days out of any twelve consecutive months.

Armed Forces Personnel: As a member of the Army, Navy, Air Force, and Coast Guard, including commissioned officers, you pay zero taxes on combat pay, hazardous duty area pay, basic living allowance, housing, travel, family education, medical treatment, GI insurance dividends, group life insurance, funeral expenses, and disability retirement pay.

A combat zone or hazardous duty area involves any location the U.S. President designates by executive order as an area in which U.S. Armed Forces are or have been engaged in combat. These areas also include military locations outside a combat zone or hazardous duty area if your services directly support military operations in the combat zone or hazardous duty area, and your service qualifies you for special military pay because of hostile fire or imminent danger.

Your estate pays zero income taxes for all earnings you received during the year of your death, provided your death occurred from your presence in a combat zone or hazardous duty area, and regardless of whether your earnings arose from work inside or outside a combat zone or hazardous duty area.

Work Transportation: You pay zero taxes for the business use of a company car or airplane, or for the non-business use of a company vehicle the IRS considers to be of limited personal value, such as certain trucks (dump, flatbed, garbage, refrigerator, delivery), hearses, farm equipment, combines, and forklifts.

As an automobile salesperson, you pay zero taxes for the business and personal use of a company demonstration vehicle, but certain restrictions apply. This vehicle may not be driven by your family, or used for a vacation, or taken on any trip exceeding seventy-five miles from your company office.

You pay zero taxes on a limited amount of money received from your employer for public transportation to and from your work, or for monthly parking. You also pay zero taxes for money received from carpool passengers.

Lodging: You pay zero taxes for lodging provided at your employer's place of business, provided you accept such lodging as a condition of your employment. Please note the following special cases—

Church Leaders—Ordained ministers, rabbis, chaplains, and cantons pay zero taxes for a housing allowance provided by their church or congregation.

Peace Corps and VISTA volunteers—These persons pay zero taxes for overseas subsistence allowances.

Teachers—They pay zero taxes for lodging near the campus.

Meals: You pay zero taxes for meals provided at your employer's place of business. Due to impossible administrative expenses, the IRS permits tax-free meals away from your employer's premises when obtained during a business related trip.

Workers' Compensation: You pay zero taxes for money received as a result of a workers' compensation claim.

Disability Pensions: You pay zero taxes for employer disability pension payments received by you for permanent physical injuries. Also, you pay zero taxes for federal government disability pension payments received by you as a military veteran or victim of a terrorist attack.

Medical Insurance: You pay zero taxes for premiums paid by your employer for medical, health, accident, and disability insurance.

Group Term Life Insurance: You pay zero taxes for premiums paid by your employer for group term life insurance that provides your beneficiaries a limited amount of death benefits in the event of your death.

Death Benefits: Your beneficiaries pay zero taxes for a limited amount of death benefits received from your employer as a result of your death.

Cross-Purchase Insurance: When two business partners own a life insurance policy one another's life, the surviving partner pays zero income taxes on the death benefits paid out as a result of the other partner's death.

Buy-Sell Insurance: When a closed corporation owns a life insurance policy that covers it's shareholders' lives, the surviving shareholders pay zero income taxes on the death benefits used to purchase the decedent shareholder's stock.

Cafeteria Plans: You pay zero taxes for monetary contributions made by your employer under a written cafeteria plan that permits you to choose between taxable and non-taxable employee benefits.

Employee Courtesy Discounts: You pay zero taxes for employee discounts on company products or services, provided these discounts do not fall below your employer's cost. These tax-free fringe benefits include airline passes, hotel lodging, and telephone services, and apply to current and retired employees, as well as their family members.

Employee Gifts: You pay zero taxes for holiday gifts received from your employer, such as a turkey at Thanksgiving, provided these gifts do not involve a substantial monetary value.

Athletic Facilities: You pay zero taxes for the value of athletic facilities provided by your employer, such as gyms, swimming pools, and golf or tennis courts, provided such athletic facilities are located on property owned or leased by your employer, and substantially all use of such facilities is restricted to employees and their families.

Dependent Care Assistance: You pay zero taxes for a limited amount of money received from your employer for child day care while you work.

Adoption Benefits: You pay zero taxes for a limited amount of money received from your employer to adopt a child.

Education

Qualified State Tuition Program: You pay zero taxes on income earned by a Qualified State Tuition Program, otherwise known as an IRS 529 plan. Here is how it works. You open an investment account, deposit a limited amount per year, then withdraw the principal and income to pay for your children or grandchildren's college education. The initial investment and subsequent income grows tax-free, and can be withdrawn tax-free for college expenditures.

Tax-free college expenditures includes tuition, fees, books, supplies, and equipment, as well as room and board if your child is at least a half-time student and resides on campus. A dollar limit applies to off campus residency.

Education Individual Retirement Account: You pay zero taxes on income earned by an Education Individual Retirement Account, otherwise known as an IRS 530 plan. This plan works similar to an IRS 529 plan, but with two key differences. First, the annual contribution is less, and second, tax-free withdrawals can pay for elementary school, junior high school, high school, and college.

Tax-free expenditures include tuition, fees, books, supplies, and equipment, as well as room and board if your child is at least a half-time student and resides on campus. A dollar limit applies to off campus residency.

Employer Educational Assistance: You pay zero taxes for tuition received from your employer for any job-related education course, whether undergraduate or postgraduate, provided such course does not satisfy your employer's minimum education standards, and does not qualify you for a new profession.

Even if an education course is not job-related, you pay zero taxes on a limited amount of money received from your employer per year for any undergraduate level course, except for courses involving sports, games, or hobbies.

Special tax treatment is received by current or retired employees of an educational institution, along with their spouse and child. They pay zero taxes for any tuition reduction received from their education institution.

Scholarships and Fellowships: You pay zero taxes for a financial scholarship received from an educational institution that maintains a regular faculty, curriculum, and enrolled body of students, provided you are a degree candidate. This tax-free benefit applies to tuition, enrollment fees, books, and supplies, but not for room and board.

Investments

Municipal Bonds: You pay zero taxes on interest received from bonds involving a state, territory, municipality, or any political subdivision. You can purchase these bonds individually or through a mutual fund. You also pay zero taxes when you exchange such bonds pursuant to a refund policy in which the municipality changes the nature of the bonds.

U.S. Savings Bonds: You pay zero "current" taxes when you rollover Series EE bonds into Series HH bonds. Your tax will be deferred until you sell the Series HH bonds.

Unit Investment Trusts: You pay zero short-term capital gains taxes on stocks purchased through a Unit Investment Trust.

With most stock mutual funds, the money managers continually purchase and sell individual stocks within the fund during any given year, thus triggering short-term capital gains taxes equal to your maximum income tax rate, even if you have not sold your mutual fund shares.

In contrast, with Unit Investment Trusts, the money managers refrain from selling any stock within the trust until after one year has passed, thus eliminating any short-term capital gains tax.

Annuity Exchange: You pay zero taxes when you exchange money or other assets for a private annuity. You also pay zero taxes when you exchange one type of private annuity for another private annuity, provided the exchange relates to the same insured, and the owner never receives any surrendered funds.

Life Insurance Exchange: You pay zero taxes when you exchange money or other assets for a life insurance policy. You also pay zero taxes when you exchange one type of life insurance policy for another life insurance policy or for a private annuity, provided the exchange relates to the same insured and the owner never receives any surrendered funds.

Transfer to Corporation: You pay zero taxes when you transfer money or other assets to a corporation, provided you own at least 80% of the corporation.

Corporate Merger: You generally pay zero taxes when you receive the stock of a new company in exchange for the stock of another company as a result of a merger between the two companies.

Retirement

Social Security Benefits: You pay zero taxes on your Social Security benefits, provided you are at least 65 years old, and your annual "provisional" income does not exceed a limited amount. Let's take a closer examination at the three age periods.

<u>Prior to Age 62</u>—You have no right to receive Social Security benefits for retirement.

<u>Age 62 to 65</u>—You have the right to receive Social Security benefits for retirement. You receive more benefits for every year after age 62 that you postpone taking them. You forfeit $1 of benefits for every $2 of income in excess of certain amount per year. Any benefits you receive may be taxed based upon your provisional income.

<u>Age 65 and older</u>—You have the right to receive Social Security benefits for retirement. You do not receive more benefits for every year after age 65 that you postpone taking them. You do not forfeit any benefits. Any benefits you receive may be taxed based upon your provisional income.

Provisional income includes wages, salaries, taxable and tax-free investment income and interest. It also includes a designated percentage your Social Security benefits when your annual gross income exceeds a certain amount.

Here are 6 ways to reduce your provisional income:

<u>Remain Single</u>—A single couple living together can earn more provisional income than a married couple without paying taxes on their Social Security benefits.

<u>Separate Homes</u>—A married couple living apart in separate residences can earn more provisional income than a married couple living together without paying taxes on their Social Security benefits.

<u>Family Limited Partnership</u>—You earn no provisional income on limited partnership interests given to your children, loved ones, and business

employees. For more details, refer to the previous discussion on Family Limited Partnerships under the caption entitled "Work."

Irrevocable Trust—You earn no provisional income on assets transferred to an irrevocable trust for the benefit of your family and loved ones, nor for an irrevocable trust created for you and someone else's benefit. You earn provisional income when you receive income from the trust.

Gifts—You earn no provisional income on appreciated assets given to your family and loved ones. However, you may pay a gift tax if your annual gifts exceed a limited amount per person.

Charitable Remainder Trust—You earn no provisional income on appreciated assets donated to an IRS approved charity or family foundation. For more details, refer to the previous discussion on Charitable Remainder Trusts under the caption entitled "Estate."

Roth IRA: You pay zero taxes on income received from a Roth IRA, provided your account has existed at least five years and you are at least 59 1/2 years old.

Two important points to remember: First, you can convert a standard IRA to a Roth IRA by paying the income taxes owed on the standard IRA, then converting it to a Roth IRA. Second, unlike a standard IRA, after age 70 ½, you need not make any mandatory withdrawals from, or stop contributing to, a Roth IRA. You can simply allow your Roth IRA to grow tax-free for an indefinite time period, even beyond your death.

In the event of your death, the balance of your Roth IRA will be paid tax-free to your heirs, even over their lifetimes if they so choose.

Estate

Inheritance: You pay zero income or estate taxes on assets you inherit from a decedent's estate.

You also receive a "stepped-up basis" on the property. For example, if an individual purchases a home for $100,000 (original basis), then sells the home for $1 million dollars, that individual might pay a capital gain tax based upon the difference between the $100,000 purchase price and $1 million sale price (i.e.-$900,000 subject to tax). However, if that individual never sold the home during his lifetime, but instead, bequeathed it to you at his death, you receive a stepped-up basis of $1 million, thus eliminating all taxes, unless you sell the home for more than $1 million.

Living Trust: Married and single persons can eliminate estate taxes by owning a Living Trust.

A married couple can double the federal estate tax exemption amount by creating a Living Trust that includes a survivor trust and exemption trust, which come into existence upon the death of one spouse.

A married couple can pay zero estate taxes on additional assets, depending upon how long the surviving spouse lives, and whether the couple implemented advanced estate planning techniques such as a Limited Family Partnership or Limited Liability Company.

Single persons can also eliminate estate taxes with a Living Trust by including a beneficiary and exemption trust, which come into existence upon the trustor's death. Estate taxes will not be eliminated upon the trustor's death, but instead, upon the death of the trustor's beneficiaries.

Married and single persons pay zero gift taxes upon the creation of a Living Trust, nor will a Living Trust increase their income or property taxes. All gains or losses from a Living Trust will be calculated on their individual tax return at their individual tax rate. They need not file any additional IRS tax forms.

A properly drafted "Living Trust Estate Plan" should contain the following legal documents: Living Trust, Certificate of Living Trust, Assignment of Assets into Living Trust, List Disposing of Tangible Personal Assets, Asset Inventory of Living Trust, Pour-Over Will, Living Will, Power of Attorney for Health Care and Financial, Title Documents, and Letter of Instruction.

Life Insurance: You pay zero income taxes on death benefits received from a decedent's life insurance policy.

Irrevocable Life Insurance Trust: Your estate pays zero estate taxes on any life insurance policy owned by this trust, provided you transferred ownership of the life insurance policy to the trust more than three years before your death, and you retain no incidents of ownership.

Family Limited Partnership: Your estate pays zero estate taxes for certain assets owned by your partnership. Please refer to the section entitled "Family" for details.

Charitable Remainder Trust: Your estate pays zero estate taxes on appreciated assets transferred to an IRS approved charity or family foundation. For more details, please refer to the above section entitled "Family."

Grantor Retained Annuity Trust: Your estate pays zero estate taxes on assets transferred to this trust. To accomplish this, you first transfer assets to a trust. Next, the trust purchases an annuity that pays you a designated income for a specific number of years. Once the trust ends, any remaining trust assets are transferred to your beneficiaries free of estate tax.

Qualified Personal Residence Trust: You estate pays zero estate taxes on the appreciated value of your personal residence. To accomplish this, you first transfer your personal residence to a trust. Next, you live rent-free at your personal residence for a specific number of years. Once the trust terminates, your personal residence will be transferred to your beneficiaries free of estate tax.

Educational Trust: Your estate pays zero estate taxes on assets transferred to a trust created for the benefit of your children or grandchildren's education.

Status

U.S. Citizen: As a U.S. citizen, you pay U.S. taxes on any income earned inside the United States. You also pay taxes on income earned outside the United States, unless you earn such income while residing in a foreign country, in which case, you can deduct a limited amount of foreign income each year on your United States tax return.

Resident Alien: A resident alien pays U.S. taxes on any income earned inside the United States. A resident alien is a non-U.S. citizen who possesses a green card or has been present in the United States 183 days or less per year.

Nonresident Alien: A nonresident alien pays zero U.S. taxes on unlimited income earned outside the United States. A Nonresident Alien also pays zero taxes on capital gains income from the sale of U.S. securities such as stocks, bonds, and mutual funds if he or she has no U.S. business.

A nonresident alien is a non-U.S. citizen who does not possess a green card nor has been present within the U.S. more than 183 days per year.

Expatriation: If you renounced your U.S. citizenship, you pay zero U.S. taxes on unlimited income earned outside the United States. An expatriate also pays zero taxes on capital gains income from the sale of U.S. securities such as stocks, bonds, and mutual funds if he or she has no U.S. business. However, if the U.S. government believes you renounced your citizenship to avoid paying future U.S. taxes, you will be required to pay U.S. taxes on income earned within and outside the U.S. for a period of 10 years after expatriation.

TAX STRATEGY # 2

Tax-Reduced Income

If you cannot find a way to convert ordinary taxable income into tax-free income, your next best alternative will be to convert ordinary taxable income into tax-reduced income. Two devices can best accomplish this tax strategy: long-Term Capital Gains income, and Tax-Sheltered income.

No tax-reduction strategy will eliminate taxes, but it can significantly lower your tax bite. How significant? Long-term capital gains tax is about half the maximum rate of ordinary taxable income, and free of FICA and FUTA taxes. As you are about to discover, Tax Sheltered income can even do better.

Long-Term Capital Gains

The IRS permits a reduced tax rate on monetary gains from capital assets. If you receive a gain from the sale or exchange of a capital asset, the amount of your taxes depends upon whether the IRS classifies your gain as short-term or long-term. The key factor is time.

Before we discuss this time factor, let's first determine what the IRS means by a "capital asset." Internal Revenue Code section 1221 states:

"The term 'capital asset' means property held by the taxpayer (whether or not connected with his trade or business), but does <u>not</u> include-

(1) stock in trade of the taxpayer or other property of a kind which would properly be included in the inventory of the taxpayer if on hand at the

close of the taxable year, or property held by the taxpayer primarily for sale to customers in the ordinary course of his trade or business;

(2) property used in his trade or business, of a character which is subject to the allowance for depreciation, or real property used in his trade or business;

(3) a copyright, a literary, musical, or artistic composition, a letter or memorandum, or similar property;

(4) accounts or notes receivable acquired in the ordinary course of trade or business for services rendered or from the sale of property;

(5) a publication of the United States Government;

(6) commodities derivative financial instruments held by commodities dealers;

(7) hedging transactions entered into in the normal course of the tax-payer's business; and

(8) supplies of a type regularly used or consumed in the ordinary course of the taxpayer's business."

In short, capital assets include real and personal property, stocks, mutual funds, even your business. Now let's look at the time factor.

When you sell a capital asset less than one year after you purchase it, any gain will be classified as a short-term capital gain. The tax rate for a short-term capital gain is easy to calculate. It's identical to your ordinary taxable income rate.

When your sale occurs more than one year after your purchase date, any gain will be classified as a long-term capital gain. The tax rate for a long-term capital gain varies between 8% and 20%, depending upon your tax bracket and the period of time you owned the capital asset. Here is the IRS tax structure:

20% for assets owned more than one year;

18% for assets purchased after December 31, 2000 and owned for more than 5 years;

15% for assets purchased after December 31, 2000 and owned for more than 5 years, provided the taxpayer is subject to a 15% income tax bracket;

10% for individuals in the 15% income tax bracket; and
8% for assets purchased after December 31, 2000 and owned for more than 5 years, provided the taxpayer is subject to a 15% income tax bracket.

Long-term capital gains are one major reason why the rich get richer, the poor get poorer, and the middle class remain middle class. Wealthy persons who receive income exclusively from the ownership of real estate and stock investments pay a maximum income tax rate of 20%. No withholding taxes, and no FICA or FUTA taxes.

Compare this 20% tax rate to an individual whose income is derived exclusively from wages. A wage earner receiving $500,000 pays more than $200,000 in taxes, whereas a long-term capital gain earner receiving the same amount pays $100,000 in taxes. That's the same income with more than twice the taxes.

The purpose of this illustration is not to criticize wealthy taxpayers who derive their income from long-term capital gains. We should all be as fortunate. The purpose of this illustration is to motivate you.

For anyone, regardless of wealth, can pursue this tax-reduction strategy. But it does not come easy. It requires discipline and time. You must invest your hard earned wages into capital assets. Eventually, with enough dedication, you too can receive the same tax relief as wealthy taxpayers.

Capital assets fall into four basic groups:

Personal Property: You can receive long-term capital gains on the purchase and sale of household furnishings, personal possessions, automobiles, and other vehicles.

Real Property: You can receive long-term capital gains on the purchase and sale of real estate, whether it involves a residence, commercial building, or raw land.

Securities: You can receive long-term capital gains on the purchase and sale of stocks, mutual funds, and bonds.

Business Assets: You can receive long-term capital gains on certain business assets described in Internal Revenue Code section 1231. These business assets include real and personal property, capital assets, crops sold with land, livestock, timber, domestic iron ore, or coal under certain conditions.

Tax Shelters

Many people believe tax shelters consist of gimmicks and legal loopholes. Nothing could be further from the truth. Ask the New York IRS office. A tax shelter syndicate recently purchased the building leased by the IRS.

Similar to tax-free income, Congress allows certain tax shelters to flourish in order to serve economic and social goals. Therefore, when you participate in a tax shelter, you not only improve your financial condition, you also further a legitimate public concern.

The Internal Revenue Code section 6111 defines a "Tax Shelter" as: "Any investment:

(1) with respect to which any person could reasonably infer, from the representations made or to be make in connection with any offer for sale of interest in the investment, that the tax shelter ratio (i.e., ration of deductions and 350% of credits to investment) for any investor may be greater than 2 to 1 as of the close of any of the first five years ending after the date on which the investment is offered for sale; and

(2) that is (i) required to be registered under federal or state law regulating securities, (ii) sold pursuant to an exemption from registration requiring the filing of notice with a federal or state agency regulating the offering or sale of securities, or (iii) a substantial investment. An investment that meets these requirements will be considered a tax shelter regardless of whether it is marketed or customarily designated as a tax shelter."

Now you know why I wrote this book. Who, with the possible exception of a very small circle of tax gurus, could ever explain this convoluted definition to an ordinary taxpayer. Believe it or not, I am about to attempt just that.

In a nutshell, a tax shelter saves you more in taxes than the money you invest in the tax shelter. All tax shelters involve one or more of the following strategies:

Tax Deferral—You accelerate deductions of land, buildings, and equipment.

Tax Leverage—You borrow money to pay for the accelerated deductions.

Tax Conversion—You convert ordinary taxable income into long-term capital gains.

Tax Credits—You receive a dollar-for-dollar reduction of taxes for the costs of land, buildings, equipment and services.

Depreciation—You receive phantom paper losses through the annual depreciation of buildings and personal property.

You most likely participated in one or more tax shelters without every realizing it. For example, if you ever bought a rental home, you most likely borrowed money to pay for the real estate; accelerated deductions for the land, building, equipment, and furnishings; depreciated the structure through phantom paper losses; received a possible tax credit if your purchase involved a community development project; and paid a 20% long-term capital gains tax when you sold the property more than one year after your purchase date. Who said Tax Shelters were gimmicks, or only reserved for risky investors?

If you enjoyed this example of a tax shelter, here are half a dozen more tax shelters that pass IRS scrutiny. We begin with the most common tax shelters, then move toward more exotic ones:

Life Insurance: A single premium life insurance policy offers a tax-free build up of cash value (tax deferral), along with a large death benefit that provides tax-free income to your beneficiaries (tax conversion).

Municipal Bond Swaps: This tax shelter allows you to receive a tax deduction on your current investment income. First, you purchase tax-free municipal bonds. If and when interest rates increase, the value of your municipal bonds will normally decrease. At this time, you swap bonds. In other words, you sell your devalued municipal bonds, wait 30 days to avoid a wash sale, then purchase equivalent municipal bonds.

You can deduct your passive bond losses against: (1) an unlimited amount of passive gains on other securities; and (2) a limited amount each year against non-passive ordinary income. You may even carry over additional bond losses to future tax years.

Equipment Leasing: The key tax benefit resulting from equipment leasing involves tax deferral and depreciation. Here is how a typical equipment lease works: First, a business entity purchases equipment with a down payment plus financing. Next, the business leases the equipment to a lessee for a designated time period and amount. The business then receives tax benefits over the lease term in the form of equipment depreciation and income tax deferral.

Cattle Feeding Programs: This tax shelter enables full time farmers to earn income during year one, and defer taxes on that income until year two at a lower tax rate. In a typical program, a farmer purchase young calves in the late summer or fall. The farmer then raises these calves in feed yards. During the next year, when the calves reach a commercial weight, the farmer sells the calves for a profit.

Cattle Breeding Programs: This tax shelter offers substantial tax deductions over a long time period. In a typical program, a tax shelter syndicate might purchase 100 cows. These cows then reproduce over three to four years to become three hundred cows. Annual maintenance costs average $12,000. The syndicate offsets these costs by the receiving an annual $6,000 tax deduction. The syndicate eventually sells the cows for a profit.

Oil and Gas: This tax shelter achieves tax reduction through an oil and gas venture that deducts the full cost of capital expenditures made during the first year. These capital expenditures involve intangible drilling and developing costs, otherwise known as IDC. A second tax benefit comes by means of a declining balance depreciation on a percentage of the remaining capitalized expenditures made during the subsequent years. If that isn't good enough, a third tax benefit occurs by taking a statutory depletion deduction based upon a percentage of gross income received from the venture.

This last investment brings up the most important fact about tax shelters: your peace of mind. Before you enter into any tax shelter, review the prospectus. Make certain the tax shelter intends to make a profit. Most importantly, scrutinize the promoter's historical performance.

Even when the tax shelter passes this examination, if you're not mentally prepared for a possible audit, stay away. Simply because Congress approves a certain tax shelter does not necessarily guarantee the IRS will refrain from auditing it for possible noncompliance.

TAX STRATEGY #3

Tax-Deferred Income

Tax-deferred income consists of earnings you decide not to currently receive, but instead, decide to receive at a future date, usually after your retirement. You pay zero "current" taxes on these earnings.

So what happens with your deferred earnings? You invest them in one or more employer or individual plans approved by the federal government. In other words, you invest these earnings in mutual funds, securities, life insurance, annuities, and real estate, and watch them grow tax-deferred.

Besides paying zero current taxes on your deferred earnings, you also pay zero current taxes on income and interest generated by your deferred earnings. You never pay taxes until the date you make a withdrawal from the plan, at which time you will pay ordinary income taxes on your earnings and on income and interest generated by your earnings.

But watch out. If you're not careful, the IRS will also require you to pay a penalty and surrender charge on your withdrawals. Fortunately, with a little extra planning, you can avoid this problem.

Qualified Plans

The federal government introduced qualified plans as a result of the Employee Retirement Income Security Act of 1974, otherwise known as ERISA. Two types of qualified plans fall under ERISA: Qualified Defined "Benefit" Plans, and Qualified Defined "Contribution" Plans.

The federal government later introduced "statutory" stock plans as a result of the Economic Recovery Tax Act of 1981, otherwise known as ERTA. Three stock plans fall under ERTA: Incentive Stock Options (ISO), Employee Stock Purchase Plans ESPP), and Employee Stock Ownership Plans (ESOP).

The forgoing plans may be compared with two other groups of tax-deferred plans known as "unqualified" and "individual" plans. Although not under the ERISA umbrella, these latter plans have passed scrutiny from Congress and the IRS. We will discuss them later.

Qualified "Benefit" Plans

Employees pay zero "current" taxes on employment earnings they decide not to currently receive, but instead, invest inside a retirement plan approved by the federal government. Tax experts often refer to these plans by their internal Revenue Code sections: 401a, 412i, 419, and a special plan named Keogh.

A Qualified Defined Benefit Plan constitutes a fixed pension plan. The Employer establishes and maintains a pension plan that designates a monetary sum an employee will receive at retirement based upon compensation and years of service. The employer then makes monetary contributions to this plan. The employee never makes any contributions. At retirement, the employee receives a guaranteed fixed sum of money for the remainder of the employee's life.

Here is an eight-point list that summarize the basic characteristics of benefit plans, including their advantages and disadvantages:

1. IRS approval—The IRS will issue a written letter of approval.

2. Business Entity—Any business entity can participate, including a Corporation, Limited Liability Company, Limited Partnership, Partnership, and Sole Proprietorship.

3. Amount—These plans allow the largest available tax deferral of earnings, in some cases exceeding $100,000 per year.

4. Asset Protection—Assets within these plans receive federal and possible state protection against an employee's unknown future creditors for claims involving negligence or breach of contract. Assets within these plans also receive protection against the employer's creditors. The employee's benefits are guaranteed at retirement.

5. Tax Deduction—While an employee receives tax deferred earnings, the employer receives an immediate tax deduction for contributions to the plan.

6. Withdrawals—To receive IRS approval, the employer must maintain the plan for at least five years, or until the employee's retirement. At retirement, the employee can normally choose one of three payout methods: lump-sum payout, lifetime income, or continued deferral to future years.

7. Nondiscriminatory—The employer must allow certain percentage of all employees to participate in the plan, but only those employees who are at least twenty-one years old, and have worked full time at the company for one to three years.

8. Ordinary Taxable Income—All money received from the plan will be considered ordinary taxable income. The employee's pension will never receive a tax-free or tax-reduced status.

Let's take a moment to view the most common plans in closer detail:
401a: An employee can defer pre-taxed employment earnings in excess of $100,000 per year. These earnings and the related investment income grow tax-free until the payout date.

To pass IRS scrutiny, an actuary reviews the plan prior to the commencement date, and at the beginning of each year. Based upon the actuarial review, the plan receives a letter of approval from the IRS.

412i: Similar to a 401a plan, an employee can defer pre-taxed employment earnings in excess of $100,000 per year. Unlike a 401a plan, earnings grow tax-free inside a fixed whole life insurance policy and/or annuity. The participating insurance company fully guarantees the employee's deferred earnings and investment.

419a: This plan provides payments to highly compensated business owners and their employees through a multiple employer trust. Payments are issued for disability and medical needs, supplement unemployment, severance compensation, and life insurance benefits.

Four key facts distinguish this plan from the preceding plans. First, all deferred earnings are invested in life insurance contracts. Second, there exists no annual monetary limit, although to insure IRS scrutiny, most employees keep death benefits lower than twenty times their annual salaries. Third, an employee forfeits the plan benefits in the event of retirement. Fourth, no penalties exist for excess contributions, accumulations, distributions, or early or late withdrawals.

Keogh: The word "Keogh" came from the name of a New York Congressman who proposed the retirement plan. Only Unincorporated businesses can establish and maintain this plan. It can be structured as a benefit plan, or more commonly, as contribution plan. Please refer to the Keogh discussion under defined contribution plans for more details.

Qualified "Contribution" Plans

In a qualified contribution plan, employees pay zero "current" taxes on employment earnings they do not receive, but instead, invest inside a retirement plan approved by the federal government. Tax experts often refer to these plans by their internal Revenue Code sections or acronyms: 401k, 403b, 457, SEP, SIMPLE, and that hybrid plan called Keogh.

Unlike benefit plans, contribution plans do not involve a fixed pension that the employer pays an employee at retirement, but instead, involve an annual contribution which the employer makes to an employee's plan until he or she quits or retires. Some of these plans require employees to make monetary contributions. At retirement, employees do not receive a guaranteed sum of money for the remainder of their lives. Instead, they receive a lump sum of money that has fluctuated in value as a result of market conditions.

To best understand contribution plans, let's view them through the same eight-point list applied to benefit plans:

1. IRS approval—The IRS will not issue a written letter of approval. Nevertheless, these plans do pass IRS scrutiny.

2. Business Entity—Most plans can be established by any business entity, including a Corporation, Limited Liability Company, Limited Partnership, Partnership, and Sole Proprietorship. Only Keogh plans are limited to an unincorporated business.

3. Amount—These plans have tight limits on the amount of annual tax-deferred earnings. This limit problem can be alleviated through a supplementary benefit plan.

4. Asset Protection—Assets within these plans receive federal and possible state protection against an employee's unknown future creditors for claims involving negligence or breach of contract. Assets within these plans also receive protection against the employer's creditors. Contributions will not be guaranteed at an employee's retirement. The employee's assets may be lost due to adverse conditions of the financial markets.

5. Tax Deduction—While an employee receives tax-deferred earnings, the employer receives an immediate tax deduction for money contributed to the plan.

6. Withdrawals—An employee cannot withdraw money from the plan prior to age 59 ½ without incurring a penalty, unless the employee satisfies one of the following five exceptions: education, medical bills, first time home purchase, death, or substantial periodically equal payments for the latter of five years or until age 59 ½. Additionally, after age 70 ½, a participant must normally withdraw a minimum amount of the total plan assets per year. Otherwise, the IRS will assess a 50% penalty on any required amounts a participant fails to withdraw from the plan.

7. Nondiscriminatory—The employer must allow a certain percentage of all employees to participate in the plan, but only those employees who are at least twenty-one years old, and who have worked full time at the company for one to three years.

8. Ordinary Taxable Income—All money withdrawn from the plan will be considered ordinary taxable income. An employee's withdrawal will never receive a tax-free or tax-reduced status.

Let's take a moment to view the most common plans in closer detail:

401k: The employer establishes and maintains a retirement plan whereby an employee deposits a limited amount of pre-taxable earnings per year. The employee pays zero taxes on the earnings until withdrawal. The employer receives an immediate tax deduction for any matching contributions the employer makes to the plan.

403b: The Employer establishes and maintains a tax-deferred annuity plan for an employee. The employer must be a nonprofit charity, or an educational or religious organization.

457: State or local government entities, or private tax-exempt organizations, establish and maintain this plan for their employees. An employee funds the plan with pre-taxed earnings, and pays zero taxes until the withdrawal date.

Simplified Employee Pension ("SEP"): The employer establishes and maintains a retirement plan whereby the employer deposits a limited amount of an employee's pre-taxable earnings per year. An employee pays zero taxes on the earnings until withdrawal, while the employer receives an immediate tax deduction.

Savings Incentive Matching Plan for Employees ("SIMPLE"): Small businesses with a limited number of employees who earn a minimum income threshold can establish and maintain a retirement plan. The rules for this plan are similar to an IRA or 401k plan.

Keogh: Only unincorporated businesses can establish and maintain a Keogh plan. It can be structured as a benefit or contribution plan. Contribution plans fall into two sub-categories.

The first sub-category is called a "Profit Sharing Contribution Plan." The employer makes annual voluntary contributions to an employee's plan, but only when the employer's company earns a profit.

The second category is called a "Money Purchase Plan." The employer makes annual mandatory contributions to an employee's plan, regardless of whether the employer's company earns an annual profit or loss.

Both plans provide identical contribution limits. Both plans permit the employer to receive an immediate tax deduction for contributions made to the plan, and also enable an employee to pay zero taxes on those contributions until the withdrawal date.

Qualified Stock Plans

As a result of the Economic Recovery Act of 1981, Congress provides special tax treatment for certain employee stock plans, otherwise known as "statutory stock options." Employees pay zero taxes on the date their employers grant them statutory stock options, and zero taxes on the date they exercise the grant by purchasing or acquiring the company stock. No taxable event occurs until the employee actually sells the company stock. Tax Experts often refer to these stock plans by their abbreviated letters: ISO, ESPP, or ESOP.

Statutory Incentive Stock Option ("ISO"): The employer "grants" an employee the right to purchase company stock. The "amount" of stock is limited. The "price" must be equal to the fair market value on the date of grant. The "date" which an employee may purchase the stock normally occurs three to five years after an employee's hiring date.

Look to three distinct dates to determine the tax treatment of an ISO. An employee pays zero taxes on the date the employer "grants" the stock option right; zero taxes on the date an employee "exercises" the option by purchasing or acquiring the stock; and a 20% long-term capital gains tax on the date the employee "sells" the stock, but only if the stock is sold more than one year after the exercise date. If sold within one year, the employee pays ordinary taxable income on any stock gain.

Statutory Employer Stock Purchase Plan (ESPP): Similar to an ISO, the employer grants an employee the right to purchase company stock. The "amount" of stock is also limited, but the "price" is normally lower than the fair market value on the date of purchase. The "date" upon which the employee may purchase the stock normally occurs three to five years after the employee's hiring date.

Look to three distinct dates to determine the tax treatment of an ESPP. Like ISO stock, an employee pays zero taxes on the date the employer "grants" the stock option right, and zero taxes on the date an employee "exercises" the option by purchasing or acquiring the stock.

Unlike ISO stock, when an employee sells the stock, he or she pays ordinary taxable income on the difference between the exercise price and the fair market value on the date of purchase or acquisition, and a 20% long-term capital gains tax on the difference between the sale price and the fair market value on the date of sale, but only if the stock is sold more than one year after the exercise date. For stock sold less than one year, an employee pays ordinary taxable income on any stock gain.

Employer Stock Ownership Plan ("ESOP"): The employer grants an employee the right to own company stock in lieu of wages and salary. The "amount" of stock is limited. The "price" usually equals the fair market value on the date of grant. The "date" is normally once a year.

Similar to ISO stock, an employee pays zero taxes on the date the employer grants the stock; zero taxes on the date he or she actually receives ownership of the stock; and 20% long-term capital gains taxes on the date of sale, but only if he or she sells the stock more than one year after receiving stock ownership. Otherwise, an employee pays ordinary taxable income on any stock gain.

Nonqualified Plans

Unlike qualified plans, nonqualified plans are not controlled by the Employee Retirement Income Security Act of 1974, otherwise known as ERISA. Nevertheless, nonqualified plans will withstand IRS scrutiny.

Employees pay zero "current" taxes on employment earnings they do not receive, but instead, place inside a deferred compensation plan established and maintained by their employers. Tax experts often refer to these plans by technical words and funny nicknames: Controlled Executive Bonus, Voluntary Deferred Compensation, Split-Dollar Life Insurance, Rabbi Trust, Secular Trust, Top Hat Plan, Golden Parachute, and Nonstatutory Stock Purchase Options.

To better understand nonqualified plans, let's view them through the same eight-point list associated with qualified plans:

1. IRS approval—The IRS will not issue a written letter of approval. Nevertheless, these plans pass IRS scrutiny.

2. Business Entity—Every business entities can participate, including a Corporation, Limited Liability Company, Limited Partnership, Partnership, and Sole Proprietorship.

3. Amount—These plans have no monetary limits on the annual amount of tax-deferred earnings. Every dollar of an employee's earnings can receive tax deferral.

4. Asset Protection—Only funded plans receive asset protection. A funded plan occurs when the employer sets aside an employee's deferred earnings in a trust or life insurance or annuity product. Only funded plans receive protections against unknown future creditor claims of an employee and employer. Only funded plans will be guaranteed at retirement.

5. Tax Deduction—With a funded plan, the employer receives an immediate tax deduction, but the employee receives immediate taxable income. With an unfunded plan, an employee receives tax-deferred income, but the employer does not receive a tax deduction until an employee receives taxable income.

6. Withdrawals—An employee can make withdrawals at any time without incurring any penalty. The employee pays ordinary taxable income on money withdrawn from the plan.

7. Nondiscriminatory—The employer may discriminate amongst employees. The employer may choose who may participate, when they may begin participation, and how much earnings they may defer to a future date.

8. Ordinary Taxable Income—All withdrawals made from the plan will be characterized as ordinary taxable income. Earnings or investment income will ever receive a tax-free or tax-reduced status.

Let's take a moment to view several unqualified plans in closer detail:

Voluntary Deferred Compensation: The employer agrees with an employee to defer present and future earnings in return for the payment of supplemental retirement income. The employee pays no current taxes on deferred earnings, and the employer receives no tax deduction until the employee receives and pays taxes on money withdrawn from the plan.

Controlled Executive Bonus: The employer agrees with an employee to defer present and future bonuses in return for the payment of supplemental retirement income or death benefits. The employer uses the bonus to purchases a Whole Life Insurance policy on the employee's life. This agreement usually results in immediate taxable income for an employee, which the employer may choose to pay, and an immediate tax deduction for the employer.

Split-Dollar Life Insurance: The employer agrees with an employee to pay all or a portion of the premium on a Whole Life Insurance Policy. Upon retirement, the employee receives the policy cash value. In the event the employee dies prior to retirement, the employer receives the policy cash value, while the employee's beneficiaries receive the policy death benefits. This agreement usually results in immediate taxable income for the employee, which the employer may choose to pay, and an immediate tax deduction for the employer.

Rabbi Trust: The employer agrees with an employee to place a certain amount of the employee's earnings in a written trust until some future date when the employee receives the earnings. This agreement normally results in tax-deferred earnings for the employee, and no tax deduction for the employer until the employee receives and pays ordinary taxable income on the earnings. Trust earnings and income are normally subject to the employer's creditors.

Secular Trust: The employer agrees with an employee to place a certain amount of an employee's earnings in a written trust until some future date when the employee receives the earnings. Unlike a Rabbi Trust, this agreement results in immediate taxable income for the employee, and an immediate tax deduction for the employer. Trust earnings are normally protected against the employer's creditors.

Top Hat Plan: The employer agrees with a select group of management or highly compensated executives to defer their earnings until some future date. This agreement usually results in immediate taxable income for the employee, and an immediate tax deduction for the employer. All earnings and investment income are subject to the employer's creditors.

Golden Parachute Plan: The employer agrees to provide extra compensation to key employees in the event of a change of control or ownership of the employer's company. Upon payment of the extra compensation, such agreements can result in an excise tax for an employee, and the loss of a deduction for the employer, to the extent of any excessive compensation

Nonstatutory Employee Stock Purchase Plan: The employer grants an employee the right to purchase company stock. The "amount" of stock is unlimited, and the "price" is normally lower than the fair market value on the date of purchase. The "date" normally requires the employee to undergo a one-year waiting period.

Nonstatutory stock plans do not receive the preferential tax treatment that Congress provides for statutory stock plans. Look to three distinct dates to determine the tax treatment of a nonstatutory stock plan. An employee pays zero taxes on the "grant" date; ordinary taxable on the difference between the exercise price and the fair market value on the date of purchase or acquisition; and a 20% long-term capital gains tax on the difference between the sale price and the fair market value on the date of sale, but only if the stock is sold more than one year after the exercise date. For stock sold within one year, an employee pays ordinary taxable income on any stock gain.

Individual Private Plans

An individual may establish and maintain a private retirement plans outside an employment setting. Such plans include an Individual Retirement Account, commonly known as an IRA, as well as annuities and life insurance.

Once again, let's view these plans through the same eight-point list associated with previous plans:

1. IRS approval—Participants in these plans do not receive a written letter of approval from the IRS, nor do these plans fall under the ERISA umbrella of protection. Nevertheless, these plans do pass IRS scrutiny.

2. Business Entity—Only individuals can establish and maintain an IRA account. Business entities can purchase annuities and life insurance policies for their employees, or to protect against financial loss in the event of an employee's death.

3. Amount—Except for an IRA, these plans have no monetary limits.

4. Asset Protection—Most states offer some asset protection against unknown future creditor claims involving negligence and breach of contract. Only a fixed annuity and life insurance policy will be guaranteed at a participant's death. Money inside an IRA, variable annuity, and variable life insurance policy may be lost due to adverse conditions of the financial markets.

5. Tax Deduction—After meeting certain requirements, IRA participants may fund their account with pre-taxed dollars. They may also receive an

immediate tax deduction for annual contributions made to their account. Annuity and life insurance owners can only fund their plans with after-taxed dollars. They do not receive a tax deduction for any contributions made to their plans.

6. Withdrawals—Participants do not incur any penalty for withdrawing cash value from a life insurance policy, unless they withdraw all of the cash value, in which case they may incur a surrender charge. Penalties for early withdrawals from an IRA or annuity, and for a late withdrawals from an IRA, may be summarized as follows:

Pre-Age 59 ½—Most plans impart a 10% penalty on any withdrawal that occurs before a participant reaches 59 ½ years old. However, no penalty will be assessed on withdrawals made prior to age 59 ½ for education, medical bills, first time home purchase, death, and substantial periodically equal payments for the latter of five years or until age 59 ½.

Age 59 ½ to age 70 ½—Participants may withdraw all of the money, some money, or no money, without incurring any penalty. Any money withdrawn will be subject to ordinary taxable income.

Age 70 ½—For an IRA, every year following age 70 ½, a participant must withdraw a minimum amount of the IRA assets. Otherwise, the IRS will assess a 50% penalty on any amount the participant fails to withdraw. For an annuity, participants may withdraw all of the money, some money, or no money, without incurring any penalty.

7. Nondiscriminatory—Any individual can establish and maintain these plans.

8. Ordinary Taxable Income—For an IRA, any money withdrawn will be characterized as ordinary taxable income. For an annuity, money treated as a return of the owner's contributions will be characterized as a tax-free

return of capital, while investment income generated by the owner's contributions will be characterized as ordinary taxable income.

Let's take a moment to view these plans in closer detail:

Individual Retirement Account: Participants pay zero "current" taxes on earnings they do not receive, but instead, place inside an Individual Retirement Account ("IRA"). Unlike most tax-deferred plans, an employer does not establish an IRA for an employee. Instead, an individual establishes an IRA outside an employment setting, but must fund the account with employment earnings. Like every tax-deferred plan, earnings inside an IRA, along with investment income generated by those earnings, grow tax-free until the withdrawal date.

Individual Private Annuity: Unlike an IRA, an individual, or business on behalf of an employee, must use taxable dollars to fund an annuity. Like an IRA, a participant pays zero "current" taxes on all contributions and investment income within the annuity until the withdrawal date.

Life Insurance: Unlike an IRA and like an annuity, an individual, or business on behalf of an employee, must use taxable dollars to fund a life insurance policy. Like an IRA and an annuity, a participant pays zero "current" taxes on all contributions and investment income.

The key benefit of owning a life insurance policy, rather than an IRA or annuity, concerns the withdrawal rules. A life insurance policyowner can make penalty-free withdrawals at anytime and, best of all, a policyowner can even make tax-free withdrawals by structuring these withdrawals as policy loans or a return of premium. A full withdrawal, however, as compared to a partial withdrawal, may result in surrender charges.

Also keep in mind that the forgoing insurance policy must be a whole life, universal life, or variable life policy. These polices should be distinguished from a "Term" life insurance policy. A term policy is similar to renting a home. You enjoy possession, but not ownership. In contrast, the forgoing policies are similar to owning a home. You enjoy both possession and ownership. Let me further explain:

Term Life Insurance—You normally pay a fixed premium for a designated number of years, and your beneficiaries receive a specific death benefit. Your policy accumulates no cash value during your lifetime.

Whole Life Insurance—Like a Term policy, you normally pay a fixed premium for a designated number of years, and your beneficiaries receive a specific death benefit. Unlike a Term policy, a Whole Life policy accumulates cash value that grows by means of fixed investments, and from which you can borrow from without penalty.

Universal Life Insurance—You pay a flexible premium for a designated number of years, and your beneficiaries receive a flexible death benefit. You also accumulate cash value that grows by means of a guaranteed or floating interest rate, and from which you can borrow from without penalty.

Variable Universal Life Insurance—You pay a flexible premium for a designated number of years, and your beneficiaries receive a flexible death benefit. You also accumulate cash value that increases or decreases as a result of your variable investment choices, and from which you can borrow from without penalty. Your variable investment choices include mutual funds, bonds, and money market investments.

This completes the first three tax strategies that comprise our Holy Grail: Maximizing tax-free, tax-reduced, and tax-deferred income. But don't stop reading. We still have seven more tax strategies remaining.

CHAPTER THREE

▼

MAXIMIZE TAXABLE EXPENSES

This chapter will teach you how to eliminate taxes by making certain you identify each and every tax adjustment, deduction, exemption, and credit you are entitled to take under the law, and then making sure you take them.

In the previous section, we looked at income. You learned to convert gross income, or what I refer to as ordinary taxable income, into special income subject to a zero or substantially reduced tax rate.

In this section, we will look at expenses. You will learn four ways to make expenses reduce your taxes. These expenses include costs associated with your business, as well as costs associated with your employment at a business. These expenses include your marital, health, and educational status, along with the number of your household dependents. These expenses include costs associated with your investments, even from moving to a new city. We'll begin with a peculiar form of expense that Congress refers to as "adjustments."

TAX STRATEGY #4

Adjustments

You can reduce your taxes by subtracting adjustments from your gross income. Think of Adjustments as another name for a special type of tax deduction, more specifically, "above the line deductions." What line? The adjusted gross income line referred to in Chapter One. Above the line deductions, in conjunction with "below the line deductions," can substantially lower your ordinary taxable income.

Whether above or below the line, every deduction becomes more valuable as your tax rate progresses higher. For individuals in the 15% tax bracket, every $1 of deductions cuts their tax liability by 15 cents. For individuals in the 35% tax bracket, every $1 of deductions cuts their tax liability by 35 cents. Restated slightly differently, for every $1,000 of deductions, the 15% taxpayer saves $150 in taxes, whereas the 35% taxpayer saves $350, more than twice the amount of the 15% taxpayer.

So what distinguishes adjustments from other deductions? Adjustments involve above the line deductions. Adjustments are subtracted from gross income to arrive at adjusted gross income. This key fact makes them more valuable than below the line deductions for two reasons.

The first reason involves a tax concept known as "phaseout." You can no longer benefit from below the line deductions when your adjusted gross income exceeds a certain monetary level. The IRS calls this level "phaseout." Adjustments can lower your adjusted gross income below this phaseout level and thus permit you to enjoy additional below the line deductions. Translation? Adjustments means more tax savings for you.

Assume for a moment your adjusted gross totals $120,000. Further assume a $100,000 phaseout level. Under this scenario, you can no longer benefit from below the line deductions because your $120,000 adjusted gross income exceeds the $100,000 phaseout level.

Now throw in $30,000 of adjustments. As a result, you can lower your adjusted gross income from $120,000 to $90,000, or $10,000 below the $100,000 phaseout level. With $90,000 in adjusted gross income, you can enjoy an additional $10,000 in previously excluded below the line deductions.

The second reason why adjustments are so valuable involves a tax concept known as a "deductible." You cannot take advantage of such below the line deductions as medical bills, charitable contributions, and casualty losses until their monetary amounts exceed a certain percentage of your adjusted gross income. The IRS calls this percentage a "deductible." Adjustments can lower your adjusted gross income and reduce your deductible threshold, thus allowing you to more below the line deductions. Translation? Adjustments mean more tax savings for you.

Once again assume your adjusted gross income totals $120,000. Further assume the deductible for your medical deductions equals $9,000, or 7.5% of your $120,000 adjusted gross income, and that your medical bills total $8,000. Under this scenario, you cannot benefit from your medical deductions because they fail to exceed the $9,000 deductible threshold.

Now throw in $30,000 of Adjustments. As a result, you can lower your adjusted gross income from $120,000 to $90,000, and thus decrease your deductible threshold from $9,000 to $6,750. With $8,000 in medical deductions, you can now enjoy an additional $1,250 in previously excluded below the line medical deductions.

Here is a list of each adjustment or, if you prefer, above the line deductions:

Trade or Business: The internal revenue code identifies every adjustment that can be obtained from a trade or business. But first you need to know what the IRS identifies as a "trade or business." In a nutshell, the ownership of a business, or the practice of a profession, are both considered a trade or business. The performance of services as an employee is not considered a trade or business.

So what constitutes a trade or business adjustment? IRS code section 162 states:

"There shall be allowed as a deduction all the ordinary and necessary expenses paid or incurred during the taxable year in carrying on any trade or business, including—

(1) a reasonable allowance for salaries or other compensation for personal services actually rendered;

(2) traveling expenses (including amounts expended for meals and lodging other than amounts which are lavish or extravagant under the circumstances) while away from home in the pursuit of a trade or business; and

(3) rentals or other payments required to be made as a condition to the continued use or possession, for the purpose of the trade or business, of property to which the taxpayer has not taken or is not taking title or in which he has no equity."

But what does "ordinary and necessary expenses" mean? Federal tax courts define "ordinary" as an expense that is common and acceptable, or reasonable and customary, in the particular business activity. Federal courts define "necessary" as an expense that is appropriate and helpful to a taxpayer's business activity. Basically, a court views the factual circumstances surrounding any expense to determine whether that expense is ordinary and necessary.

There are literally hundreds of ordinary and necessary trade or business adjustments that can be deducted from your gross income to arrive at adjusted gross income. I have lumped them into a dozen major categories.

Start-Up Costs—You can deduct expenses associated with getting your business underway, provided you subsequently engage in that business for profit.

Operating Costs—You can deduct expenses relative to running a business, including the cost of goods and services sold, lease and rent payments, equipment, computers, furniture, supplies, marketing, advertising, telephone, fax, internet access, postage, subscriptions, insurance, and legal and accounting fees.

Home Office—You can deduct expenses associated with the use of your home as a business, but only that portion of your home used exclusively on a regular basis as a principal place of business for meeting patients, clients, or customers. "Principal place of business" includes administrative or management activities if no other place exists to perform these activities. In summary, to receive this "high audit" deduction, a specific area of your home must be used solely for business.

Compensation—Business owners can deduct a reasonable allowance for salaries, wages, or other compensation paid to their employees. This deduction includes employee bonuses, fringe benefits, retirement plans, life insurance premiums, and disability payments. Earnings paid to working relatives may be deducted if their services are needed, and these services would have been performed by an unrelated third party.

Employee Expenses—Business owners can deduct reimbursements made to employees for work related expenditures.

Travel—Whether your can deduct travel expenses depends upon the location of your principal place of business, and the time and nature of your travel.

Local Commute: Generally speaking, you cannot deduct the cost of traveling to and from your home and your primary place of employment. On the other hand, you can deduct this cost if you incur additional expenses for transporting work tools or material, or if your home is your primary place of employment, and you travel to another work location. You can also deduct the cost of traveling from an office away from your home to a temporary work site. "Temporary" means less than one year. When permitted, a vehicle deduction will be based upon a flat mileage rate or the cost of service and repair.

U.S. Travel: Besides vehicle costs, you can deduct additional expenses incurred away from your office in the pursuit of your business, but only if work duties require you to be away from your office for a temporary period that is substantially longer than one work day. Additional travel expenses include meals, lodging, and telephone calls. An expense allocation based upon time will be required for trips involving both business and pleasure.

Foreign Travel: You can deduct even more travel expenses for trips outside the United States. These expenses include air travel, taxis, and buses. Similar to U.S. travel, foreign expenses also require a time allocation between business and pleasure.

Entertainment—You can deduct 50% of any expenses incurred to entertain an existing or potential business relationship, provided you engage in an active business discussion or activity with the principal purpose of obtaining income or a specific business benefit. Entertainment deductions include those expenses directly preceding or proceeding a business discussion or activity. No deduction will be allowed for costs associated with sporting activities, except for recreational facilities used primarily for the employees' benefit, nor will a deduction be allowed for club dues.

Meals—You can deduct 50% of business meal expenses, provided you satisfy the same requirements outlined in the foregoing "entertainment" category.

Gifts—You can deduct a small business gift per recipient.

Awards—Business owners can receive a limited deduction for the cost of an employee achievement award. The award must involve tangible personal property given to an employee for length of services or safety. The amount of this deductible depends upon whether the award arose out of a qualified or a nonqualified award plan. A qualified award provides a larger deduction. It requires a written plan that does not discriminate in favor of highly compensated employees.

Charitable Contributions—Business owners can deduct the cost of a contribution or gift to an IRS approved charity, but this deduction is limited to 10% of the taxable income of the business. Any costs exceeding 10% can be carried over for five consecutive years.

Health Insurance—Self-employed individuals can deduct a large portion of health insurance premiums paid on behalf of themselves and their family.

Taxes—You can deduct state, local, and foreign taxes to the extent these taxes directly relate to your business. This deduction includes FICA

(Medicaid and Social Security) and FUTA (Unemployment and Disability) taxes paid on behalf of their employees. You can also deduct one-half of your federal self-employment taxes.

Interest—You can deduct interest related to most business activities, including loans and the production of rental or royalty income. However, you cannot deduct interest assessed on your personal income tax return, even when this interest relates to income derived from your business or trade.

Uniform—You can deduct the purchase and upkeep costs of a uniform or special article of clothing, provided such clothing is required as a condition of your employment and it cannot be worn in public during non-working hours. This rule has several exceptions, including work shoes and gloves.

Rental Property: You can deduct expenses attributable to rental properties.

Royalty Property: You can deduct expenses attributable to royalty properties.

Employee Reimbursed Expenses: You can deduct any expenses for which you received reimbursement from your employer pursuant to a reimbursement and allowance plan established by your employer.

Special tax rules pertain to performance artists and government officials. Performance artists, including actors, can deduct any ordinary and necessary business expenses, regardless of employer reimbursement, provided they have worked two years in the performance arts business. Fee-based state or local government officials can deduct expenses paid or incurred in their employment, regardless of employer reimbursement.

Retirement Plans: Certain individuals can deduct a limited amount of payments made to a retirement savings plan, including an IRA and Keogh. Employers and self-employed individuals can deduct a limit amount of monetary contributions made to pensions, profit sharing, and annuity plans.

Premature Withdrawal Penalties: You can deduct interest forfeited to a bank and savings association on premature withdrawals from time savings accounts or deposits.

Jury Duty Pay: You can deduct jury pay you received from a court and remitted to your employer.

Medical Savings Accounts: You can deduct contributions made to a medical savings account established and maintained by your employer.

Trusts: You can deduct certain repayments of supplemental unemployment compensation benefits made to a trust. A life tenant or income beneficiary of property held in trust can receive a depreciation and depletion allowance.

Education Loan Interest: You can deduct interest paid on student loans during the first sixty months of the loan.

Moving Expenses: You can deduct certain moving expenses necessary to change job locations, provided your new job location is at least fifty miles away from your former job location; you move within one year of changing jobs; and you work full time at this new job at least thirty-nine weeks during the twelve month period following your move. Deductible moving expenses include costs for travel, shipping of household goods, house hunting, temporary living, and the sale and purchase of an old and new home.

Alimony: You can deduct support payments made to your former spouse, provided such payments discharge a legal obligation made pursuant to a court order, divorce decree, or legal separation.

Fuel: You can deduct expenses incurred for the purchase of clean-fuel vehicles and refueling property.

This completes our study of adjustments, otherwise known as "above the line deductions." Now we'll focus upon "below the line" deductions, otherwise known as "itemized deductions."

TAX STRATEGY #5

Deductions

Everyone loves deductions. How many times have you heard a business owner at a restaurant say with a big smile: "Oh, don't worry about the $100 lunch bill. I'm gonna write it off." You would almost believe he didn't pay a single penny. The IRS got stuck with the tab instead.

But what really happens when you "write-off" something? Does your deduction really eliminate all out-of-pocket costs? Do you truly enjoy a free ride on Uncle Sam?

Unfortunately, the answer to these last two questions is a big fat "no," yet deductions do provide something, and something is always better than nothing.

Here's what I mean. Every deduction saves you taxes, up to a certain point. For example, the IRS permits you to deduct 100% of your home mortgage interest. Assume for a moment your annual interest totals $10,000. Also assume your in a 35% tax bracket. By receiving this deduction, you save $3,500 in taxes, or 35% of the $10,000 interest payment. That's $3,500 more than you would have received without the deduction, but you never recapture the remaining $6,500 balance of your $10,000 mortgage interest payment. It's still a pretty good deal. This deduction does not eliminate interest payments, but it certainly eliminates thousands of dollars in taxes.

Now let's return to that smiling business owner who paid $100 for a work-related lunch. In this case, the IRS only permits him to deduct 50% of the bill. Assuming the same 35% tax bracket used in our previous example, by receiving this deduction, our business owner merely saves $17.50, or 17.5% of $100. That's just half the percentage you received for your home mortgage interest. Our business owner will never recapture the remaining $82.50 of his $100 business lunch. It's no longer a pretty good deal, but it's better than nothing.

Finally, let's assume you and our business owner have adjusted gross incomes in excess of that dreaded "phaseout" level when all hell breaks loose. At this point, all of your beloved deductions do a hocus pocus disappearing act. They become worthless. 100% of the mortgage interest and lunch bill are paid without any tax savings. It's not a pretty good deal. It's not even better than nothing. In fact, it is nothing.

What I'm attempting to say is quite simple. Tax deductions cannot compete with tax-free income nor, as you'll soon learn, with tax credits, but tax deductions will lower your tax liability, at least until you reach that God forsaken phaseout point.

Just as we saw with adjustments, deductions become more valuable as your tax bracket goes higher and higher. A 35% taxpayer saves $35 for every $100 of deductions, whereas a 15% taxpayer saves only $15. Who ever taught rich individuals how to become richer certainly knew about the power of tax deductions.

But what about the poor and middle class taxpayers? Fortunately, they too can benefit from tax deductions. That's because a large percentage of deductions are available to nearly everyone. In fact, Congress provides each and every taxpayer one particular deduction that translates into thousands of dollars of tax savings. Congress calls it the "standard deduction."

Promoters of tax deductions contend that deductions give Congress the power to promote and regulate social and economical activities that benefit our nation. Critics of tax deductions claim that deductions merely constitute a payback to certain powerful lobbies and interest groups. After reading hundreds of pages of tax deductions in the IRS tax code, I would agree with both arguments. But don't just take my word. Judge for yourself.

Standard Deduction: Congress provides everyone with a precise dollar amount of deductions based upon his or her filing status. Congress calls it the standard deduction. You simply compare this standard deduction against the total dollar amount of your itemized deductions, then use whichever amount is greater. We will discuss one's filing status in the tax strategy #6 entitled "Exemptions." In the meantime, your filing status will be either: Married Filing Jointly, Married Filing Separately, Qualifying Widow, Head of Household, or Single.

Income Production: You can deduct any ordinary and necessary expenses paid or incurred for the production or collection of income, and for the maintenance, management, and conservation of property held for the production of income.

Examples of these deductions include investment fees for attorneys, custodians, and clerical help; office rent; state and local transfer taxes; fees attributable to property held for the production of rents and royalties; depreciation and depletion of a life tenant's estate; costs associated with the guardianship or ward of a minor; expenses incurred to determine or collect any tax; and legal expense for the production of income, or the maintenance and management of income producing property or the recovery of investment property.

Employee Unreimbursed Expenses: You can deduct work-related expenses for which you receive no reimbursement from your employer, but not until these expenses exceed 2% of your adjusted gross income. For instance, if you earn an annual income of $50,000, you receive no tax benefit for any unreimbursed work-related expenses not exceeding $1,000.

Medical Expenses: You can deduct medical bills from your adjusted gross income, but not until these bills exceed 7.5% of your adjusted gross income. This deduction includes personal medical bills, as well as medical bills paid on behalf of your spouse or dependents.

And what does the IRS mean by the term "medical bills?" The IRS code and court cases have permitted deductions for medical bills pertaining to any payment made for the purpose of affecting any structure or function of your body; treatment of specific diseases; qualified long-term care services; medicine and drugs; smoking cessation program; birth control and abortion costs; certain psychiatric treatment; premiums paid for medical insurance; weight reduction programs to improve your general health; transportation costs primarily for and essential to medical care; lodging, but not meals, when necessary to visit a medical provider; expenses incurred by a person who must accompany you to a medical provider; even certain home improvements made primarily for medical purposes.

Charitable Contributions: You can deduct any charitable contributions from your adjusted gross income, but only to the extent these contributions exceed a certain percentage of your contribution base.

Your "contribution base" normally equals your adjusted gross income. We previously learned that adjusted gross income equals your gross income minus adjustments.

Two factors determine the "percentage" of your contribution base that can be deducted from your adjusted gross income: the type of property donated, and the type of charitable organization. You can deduct 50% of any charitable contribution made to an IRS recognized tax-exempt organization. You can also deduct 30% of any charitable gift of appreciated property. Any unused deduction may be carried forward for five successive tax years.

Casualty Losses: You can deduct non-business losses from your adjusted gross income, but only to the extent these losses exceed a $100 deductible threshold, and 10% of your adjusted gross income.

Non-business casualty losses include sudden and unexpected damage resulting from: fire, storm, shipwreck, theft, embezzlement, automobile collision or motorcycle accident, the insolvency of a financial institution, and a hobby engaged in for profit to the extent of income produced by the hobby. You cannot deduct any monetary loss arising from the sale of your residential or vacation home.

Gambling Losses: You can deduct gambling losses from your adjusted gross income, but only to the extent of your gambling winnings.

Taxes: You may deduct state, local, and foreign real property taxes; state and local personal property taxes, including payment for the registration of a vehicle if imposed annually and assessed in proportion to the vehicle value; state, local, and foreign income taxes, war profits, or excess profit tax; and any generation skipping transfer tax imposed on income distributions.

You cannot deduct federal income taxes; social security taxes; one-half of your self-employment taxes; federal war profits and excess profit taxes; estate, inheritance, legacy, succession, and gift taxes; or improvement taxes such as assessments made for local benefits, including streets, sidewalks, and other like improvements, unless levied for maintenance.

Interest: You can deduct interest paid for certain loans against adjusted gross income, such as a home equity mortgage; prepaid home interest, normally referred to as "points;" educational loan interest; and stock margin interest. To qualify, the loan must involve a legally enforceable contract.

You cannot deduct any interest involving investment indebtedness; life insurance; personal interest; or a loan to purchase and carry tax-exempt securities.

Education: You can deduct any education costs, so long as the education meets, maintains, or improves a skill required in your employment, profession, trade, or business.

You cannot deduct education expense that satisfy a minimal educational requirement of your employment, trade, or business, or qualifies you for a new profession, trade, or business.

Dues: You can deduct union dues, initiation fees, and out-of-work benefit assessments, but not professional association fees.

Vacation Home: You receive a limited deduction for costs associated with a vacation home, but only if you rent this home more than 14 days per year, or 10% of the rental days available per year. If you take this deduction, you must also include all rental fees as ordinary taxable income.

This completes our study of itemized deductions, otherwise known as "below the line deductions." Now we'll turn our attention upon your marital status and residential dependents, otherwise known as "exemptions."

TAX STRATEGY #6

Exemptions

You can realize significant tax savings by minimizing the estimated taxes withheld from your paycheck, or in the event you're self-employed or retired, by minimizing the estimated quarterly taxes you pay the IRS. How can you accomplish this? By determining your applicable "filing status," and the correct number of your "dependents." The IRS calls this determination your "exemptions."

Now some people might say: "I like overestimating my withholding taxes throughout the year. That way I receive a nice big refund on April 15th. It's like getting a present from Uncle Sam."

Wrong. By paying Uncle Sam too many tax dollars throughout the year, you allow Uncle Sam to earn interest on your hard-earned money. By paying Uncle Sam the correct amount, you earn interest on your money. Translation? More dollars in your pocket each year.

Now some people might still say: "I understand what you're telling me, but I don't want to follow your advice. If I stopped overestimating my tax payments, I would never invest the saved money. I'd simply spend it. By entrusting Uncle Sam with some extra money during the year, I get use to living without it, and when everyone else sends tax payments on April 15th, I receive a tax refund instead."

Yes, indeed, you must exercise discipline to make this tax strategy work. I just want you to remember one important point. Let's say you overpay Uncle Sam $5,000 through withholding taxes every year. Do you want

Uncle Sam receiving the extra $350 of interest generated by your overpayment? Couldn't you use that extra money? Decide for yourself.

If you have no discipline, yet still want to earn interest on your money, try this alternative. Designate your correct number of exemptions, then have your employer place the money you normally overpay Uncle Sam in a deferred compensation plan. At least you won't spend the extra dollars throughout the year, and your money grows tax-free until you decide to withdraw it.

Exemptions reduce withholding taxes to a bare minimum. To determine your correct number of exemptions, you must focus upon two factors: filing status and dependents. Here we go, one at a time.

Filing Status

Every taxpayer must designate a filing status on his or her tax return. The IRS limits your selection to one of five categories: married filing jointly, married filing separately, head of household, qualifying widow, or single.

Your Filing Status plays two vital roles in reducing taxes. The first role concerns the standard deduction, or the minimum income level beneath which you pay no taxes. Married couples receive a larger standard deduction than single persons. An identical amount of income can require a single person to pay taxes while a married couple pays none.

The second role concerns the tax tables, or the IRS chart used to determine the tax rate on your income. Married couples receive a lower progressive tax rate than single persons. An identical amount of income can require a married couple to pay a 28% tax while a single person must pay a 31% tax.

So how do you determine your filing status? Filing status comes in five flavors. Let's begin with the category that normally provides the most beneficial tax rates, then work our way down to the category that usually provides the worst tax rates. You may have more than one flavor to choose from. Choose carefully.

Married Filing Jointly: To qualify for this category, on the final day of the tax year, you must be married, and you must file a joint tax return that includes both spouse's income. If you file separate tax returns, then your filing status becomes Married Filing Separately. Married couples can never file as Single or Head of Household.

When might a spouse consider Married Filing Separately instead of Married Filing Jointly? If one spouse has a large amount of deductions, choosing Married Filing Jointly can possibly phaseout these deductions. These same deductions may be captured by choosing Married Filing Separately.

You might also consider Married Filing Separately when your spouse has intentionally cheated the IRS out of taxes. In such case, the IRS will hold you jointly liable for the taxes, penalties, and interest owed by your spouse, unless you chose Married Filing Separately or prevail on an Innocent Spouse Relief claim.

Qualifying Widow or Widower: To qualify for this category, your spouse must have died during the year, and you must have supported a child in your household during that year. In such case, you may use the married filing jointly tax rates for the next two years. Alternatively, you may file as Single or Head of Household.

Head of Household: To qualify for this category, on the final day of the tax year, you must be single, you must provide financial support for one or more children or parents, and you must file a tax return that only includes your income.

Single: To qualify for this category, on the final day of the tax year, you must be single, and you must file a tax return that only includes your income.

Married Filing Separately: To qualify for this category, on the final day of the year, you must be married, and both spouses must file separate tax returns for their respective incomes. Please refer to Married Filing Jointly for two advantages in choosing this filing status.

Seniors and Disabled Persons: In addition to the forgoing five categories, Congress provides an additional tax rate reduction for senior citizens over age 65, and for blind or disabled individuals. These individuals must still decide amongst the five listed categories, but they receive a higher standard deduction, along with an extra tax credit.

Dependents

Dependent children running around your house translate into tax savings for you and your spouse. A dependant generally involves someone related to you by blood, or to a member of your household, for whom you provide domestic and financial support during the year.

What tax rules apply to dependents? You receive one personal exemption, that is, a specific amount of tax savings, for every Dependent. One exemption for you, one for your spouse, one for each child, and one for every parent, grandparent, grandchild, or other relative residing in your household.

There exists no limit on the number of possible dependents, only a limit on your personal sanity. More dependents means more exemptions which means more tax savings.

Can your family member answer "yes" to the following five questions? If so, congratulations! You have a dependent on your hands.

1. Relationship: Is this individual a relative of someone residing in your household? Almost any blood relative counts, even an adopted child. A member of your household must use your home as his or her principal place of dwelling.

2. Support: Does this individual receive over one-half of his or her financial support from you during the calendar year? Support includes food, shelter, and clothing, as well as medical, dental, education, and religious care. It does not include the financial value of your household services.

3. Income: Does this individual receive a small annual income? No income limit applies to children under age 19, or to children who are students under age 24. They may receive an unlimited amount of income and still qualify for dependent status.

4. Joint Tax Return: Did this individual refrain from filing a joint marital tax return? The only exception involves a dependent who filed a joint marital tax return in order to obtain a refund of withholding taxes.

5. U.S. Status: Is this individual a U.S. citizen, or resident of the United States, Canada, or Mexico at some time during the calendar year?

This completes our examination of exemptions, but don't stop reading, the final and most powerful tax strategy contained in this Chapter is yet to come. We have just seen how adjustments, deductions, and exemptions indirectly reduce your taxes by reducing your taxable income. But our next strategy directly reduces your taxes, in most cases regardless of your income. The IRS calls this strategy "tax credits." You might call this strategy manna from heaven.

TAX STRATEGY #7

Credits

You're going to develop a great fondness for tax credits. Every dollar of tax credits cuts your tax liability by one dollar, or dollar for dollar. Only tax-free income can match this feat.

To better understand the awesome power of tax credits, let's compare them to tax deductions. Whereas a deduction cuts your taxable income, a credit cuts your tax liability. Let's suppose your income falls within the 35% tax bracket. Every dollar of deductions cuts your tax liability by Thirty-five cents. In comparison, every dollar of credits cuts your tax liability by the full dollar. Do the math. A tax credit puts 65% more in your pocket than a deduction.

Please don't misunderstand me. I love deductions. Any deduction beats no deduction, but credits work for you like supercharged deductions, only much better.

Here is a list of every conceivable tax credit granted by Congress. Unfortunately, most of them go to special interest groups. But who knows? You might be a member of one such group.

Child: You receive a tax credit for each child, stepchild, grandchild, or great-grandchild under age twenty-five whom you claim as a dependent.

Adoption: You receive a tax credit for money paid to adopt a child under age eighteen, or any age if the person is mentally or physically incapable of self-care. This credit increases for a special needs child. The credit will be reduced by the amount of any employer reimbursement.

Dependent Care: You receive a tax credit for money you pay someone to care for your children at home while you're away at work. The amount of this credit depends upon the number of your children, and your annual income. This credit will be reduced by the amount of any employer reimbursement.

Earned Income: You receive a tax credit when your annual earnings fall below a specific sum of money. It's the only tax credit the IRS makes available even if you pay no taxes.

The amount of this tax credit depends upon your annual earnings, and the number of qualifying children in your home. A qualifying child includes a son, daughter, adopted child, grandchild, or stepchild who is under age nineteen, or under age twenty-four if a full-time student, or any age if permanently and totally disabled. Even if you have no children, you can still receive this tax credit, provided your annual earnings fall below a specific base amount.

Education: You can receive only one of the following two education credits during any given year. The Hope Credit allows you to receive a tax credit for college tuition and fees incurred by you, your spouse, and your dependent child. The main restriction concerns the college year. Only the first and second college years apply.

The Lifetime Learning Credit allows you to receive a tax credit for the same persons as the Hope Credit, but it permits tuition and fees for any year of college.

Elderly: You receive a tax credit if you are at least sixty-five years old.

Disabled: You receive a tax credit if you are currently retired, and were rendered permanently and totally disabled when you retired, regardless of your age.

Taxes: You receive a tax credit for federal and state taxes you paid during the year. You receive a tax credit for excess Social Security taxes you paid as a result of working for more than one employer. You receive a tax credit for any foreign income taxes you paid to a country outside the United States. You may receive a tax credit for a prior year minimum tax liability ("AMT" tax), and for tax-exempt interest on private activity bonds.

An employer receives a tax credit for income and social security taxes withheld from an employee's earnings. A corporation receives a tax credit for capital gains tax paid on undistributed capital gains.

Housing: You receive a tax credit for a portion of the interest on a home mortgage under special state and local programs. You may also receive a tax credit for money spent on the construction, rehabilitation, or purchase of a qualified low-income housing project.

Building: You receive a tax credit for investments in a qualified rehabilitated building.

Community Development: You receive a tax credit for cash contributions, including loans or investments, made to a corporation created for the development of a community.

Vehicles: You receive a tax credit for certain costs associated with the purchase of a vehicle powered by rechargeable batteries, fuel cells, or any other portable source of electric current.

Disabled Access: You receive a tax credit for expenditures that make a business accessible to disabled individuals as required by the American with Disabilities act of 1990.

Employment: Employers in the food and beverage industry receive a tax credit for a portion of social security taxes paid on employee cash tips.

Employers receive a tax credit for wages paid to employees who reside in an empowerment zone designated by the Secretary of Housing and Urban Development, or by the Secretary of Agriculture.

Employers receive a tax credit for wages paid to certain target groups, including families with dependent children, long-term family assistant recipients, veterans, ex-felons, high risk youths, summer youth employees, social security recipients, food stamp recipients, vocational rehabilitation employees, and enrolled members of Indian tribes.

Research: You receive a tax credit for incremental research expenses related to the fields of social sciences, arts and humanities, or subsidized research activities, provided such research is technological in nature and useful in developing new or improved business components. You also receive a tax credit for qualified clinical testing of new "orphan" drugs.

Electricity: You receive a tax credit for domestic production of electricity from qualified energy resources (i.e.-closed loop biomass, windmill, and poultry waste facilities).

Fuel: You receive a tax credit for cash spent on alcohol, ethanol, or qualified fuel mixtures used or sold in a fuel producer's business or trade. You receive a tax credit for money spent on enhanced oil recovery projects that increase the amount of crude oil on the open market. You receive a tax credit for federal excise taxes paid on special fuels used for farming, school buses, and in a trade or business. You receive a tax credit for the domestic production of oil, gas, and synthetic fuels created from unconventional sources, such as shale, tar sands, coal seams, and geopressured brine, provided you sell these fuels to persons unrelated to you.

Energy Equipment: You receive a tax credit for investments in energy equipment which use solar energy to generate electricity, to heat or cool a structure, or to provide solar energy derived from geothermal deposits.

Timber: You receive a tax credit for investments in commercial timber woodlands within the United States, including expenses incurred for site preparation, seeds, labor, tools, and machinery and equipment.

This completes the next four tax strategies that comprise our Holy Grail: maximizing adjustments, deductions, exemptions, and credits. But don't stop reading. Only three more strategies remain, and they all share one common element: tax shifting.

Chapter FOUR

▼

Shift Taxable Income and Expenses

Amazing as it might sound, you can control the tax year which best serves your receipt of taxable income and deductions. You can also control the individual who receives this taxable income. So goes the final tax strategy of our Holy Grail.

Before we go any further, let me share three important tax-shifting concepts: constructive receipt, cash versus accrual method taxpayers, and year-end tax planning.

What does constructive receipt mean? Simply stated, you cannot avoid taxation by simply refusing to cash a paycheck, or by refusing to accept income you earned and may receive without restrictions. Nor can you avoid taxation by assigning or transferring this income to another person.

Nevertheless, through careful tax shifting plans, you can avoid constructive receipt of earned income in the current year. It's not just a matter of semantics. It's a matter of making advance planning choices that pass IRS scrutiny and result in tax savings for you and your family.

What distinguishes a cash method taxpayer from an accrual method taxpayer? The overwhelming majority of Americans are cash method taxpayers. These taxpayers trigger a taxable event when they receive income or pay expenses.

In contrast, accrual method taxpayers trigger taxable events when they earn income or owe expenses. Income may therefore be taxed prior to receipt, and expenses deducted prior to payment. Income shifting techniques normally require a cash method taxpayer.

One unique event triggers the same tax consequence for cash and accrual method taxpayers. Purchases made with credit cards. Such purchases trigger a taxable event on the charge date, even if the taxpayer postpones payment of the bill until the following year.

What do we mean by year-end tax planning? The following tax shifting strategies require you to plan far in advance of December, although you pull the trigger in December.

TAX STRATEGY #8

Shift Income
to Future Tax Years

This beloved strategy involves shifting taxable income from the current year to a future year. When would you do this? When income received in the current year would be subject to a higher tax bracket, or would phase-out deductions, than if such income was received in a future year. Why would you do this? To pay less taxes. The tax savings between the two years goes into your pocket instead of into Uncle Sam's pocket.

The following strategies will successfully shift income of a cash method taxpayer to a future tax year.

<u>Wages and Salary:</u> You might ask your employer to defer until next year any income, bonus, or severance payments. Just remember, you cannot delay taxes by simply waiting until the beginning of next year to cash or deposit a paycheck. Nor can you delay taxes by merely postponing receipt of a paycheck. To properly delay taxes, your employer must agree to issue your paycheck next year, and this agreement must take place before the date you render services that earn you that paycheck.

<u>Business Sales:</u> As a business owner, you might wait until next year to mail customer invoices for services you performed or products you sold this year. You might also wait to collect any account receivables.

<u>Investments:</u> You might delay until next year the sale of appreciated stocks, bonds, mutual funds, or personal or real property. Until the time of sale, no taxable event occurs on investment gains, with the exception of issued dividends.

On the other hand, if you hold a mixed bag of assets, only some of which reveal a potential gain, you might consider eliminating taxes in the current year by selling an equal amount of gains and losses before next year. Just make certain to sell any stocks by December 29th, and make certain to match passive income against passes losses.

Why December 29th? The IRS considers any sale after December 29th to be a taxable event in the next tax year. The stock transaction may occur on December 29th, but it does not settle until the following year.

Why match passive income against passive losses? The IRS makes a distinction between certain kinds of income and losses. Passive income or loss involves stocks or real estate, property that is subject to short-term and long-term capital gains taxes. Non-passive income or loss involves wages or salaries, earnings that are subject to ordinary taxable income. The IRS permits an unlimited amount of passive losses to be offset against passive income, but it severely limits the amount of passive losses that can be offset against non-passive income. You must also match short-term passive gains against short-term passive losses, and long-term passive gains against long-term passive losses.

Another investment income shifting technique involves your purchase of U.S. treasury bills, savings certificates, and government or private bonds after July 1st. These investments will not trigger any taxable event until the following year, so long as their income and interest carry a six to twelve month maturity date.

Contracts: You might consider a monthly installment contract that extends into future years, instead of a one-time payment contract. You might also consider extending until next year the payment date on any contract that provides you monthly income, such as a loan, first trust deed, or installment note.

Retirement Plans: You might consider setting up one or more retirement plans, including a qualified defined benefit or contribution plan, non-qualified plan, stock plan, or individual retirement account. In fact, most plans can be established in the current year, funded before April 15th of the following year, and still provide you with a tax deduction in the current year.

TAX STRATEGY #9

Shift Income to Other Taxpayers

Another excellent tax reduction strategy involves the shifting of income from an individual in a high tax bracket to an individual in a lower tax bracket. Family members commonly implement this income shifting technique through the use of gifts, employment earnings, and co-ownership of a business.

I have broken down this strategy into four categories: minors, spouse, other adults, and shared business ownership.

<u>Minors</u>: Congress distinguishes two categories for minors: minors under age fourteen, and minors age fourteen and older. Congress created a special tax treatment for minors under age fourteen, and called it the "kiddie tax."

<u>Tax Rates</u>—Income received by a minor less than fourteen years old will be subject to the kiddie tax if such income constitutes unearned income instead of earned income. Earned income means income received as compensation for personal services. Unearned income means income received from any other source, including investments, property ownership, even ownership of a business.

Congress taxes a minor's earned income the exact same way as an adult's income, regardless of the minor's age. The IRS collects taxes based upon a progressive tax rate structure.

Congress taxes the unearned income of a minor less than fourteen years old according to a three-tier structure known as the "kiddie tax." A very limited amount of unearned income triggers no taxes. A certain amount of additional unearned income triggers a tax based upon the standard progressive rate structure. Any further unearned income triggers a tax based upon the minor parent's maximum tax rate. If a parent has two or more kiddies, all of the kiddies' unearned incomes will be added together, reallocated according to each kiddie's pro rata share, then taxed at the parent's maximum tax rate.

By enacting this kiddie tax, Congress tried to eliminate a parent's ability to gain a tax advantage through the shifting of income to their children. Despite this aggressive effort by Congress, numerous income-shifting strategies remain intact, backed by federal court rulings.

Gifts—You may give each minor child an unlimited amount of money or assets each year as a gift without your child incurring any income tax liability.

You may, however, be subject to gift and estate taxes. At your death, the IRS will add up all your lifetime gifts in excess of a limited amount per year, along with the fair market value of your assets, and if the combined dollar value exceeds the federal exemption limit, your estate pays a gift and estate tax.

Earned Income—Your minor children can receive earned income from your business, or from someone else's business, without any tax liability, so long as their earnings do not exceed the standard deduction threshold applicable to all adult taxpayers. Courts have allowed children as young as seven years old to receive salaries from their parents for simple work-related chores like cleaning the business or answering telephones.

Even if your children's earnings exceed the standard deduction, and thus require them to pay taxes, the use of income shifting strategies can still work to your financial advantage. For instance, let's assume you own a business, and that your income places you in the 35% tax bracket. You can employ your children, pay them reasonable salaries for their work, and still come out ahead. How?

First of all, Congress does not require a parental employer to pay FICA taxes for services performed by their children under age 18. Nor will FUTA taxes be assessed on children under age 21. Therefore, by placing your children on the family business payroll, you save FICA and FUTA taxes.

Second, when you pay your children's living expenses, every dollar paid is subject to your maximum tax rate instead of their lower tax rate. If, for example, you occupy a 35% tax bracket, you retain only sixty-five cents from every dollar earned to purchase your children's clothes, food, entertainment, education, or whatever else they need.

Now assume your children occupy a 15% tax bracket. In such case, you would retain eighty-five cents from every dollar earned to pay for these very same living expenses. The ultimate result? Your purchasing power increases by as much as twenty cents, or 20%, for every dollar earned.

Individual Retirement Account—To really leverage the preceding income shifting strategy, open Individual Retirement Accounts in your children's names, then fund these accounts with your children's earnings. You have now designed a double-barrel shotgun. The earnings which fund the accounts will not be subject to current taxation, and all future investment income inside the accounts grows tax-free until the withdrawal date.

Unearned Income—You can give your minor children assets that generate unearned income without any tax liability, so long as this income does not trigger the kiddie tax threshold. Over the course of eighteen years, this strategy can generate tens of thousands of tax-free dollars.

<u>Bonds</u>—You can give your minor children Series EE U.S. savings bonds that mature after your children reach age 14. In addition, give your children tax-free municipal bonds or bonds with deep discounts. The IRS collects no taxes until your children redeem the bonds at maturity.

<u>Stocks</u>—You can give your minor children stocks or mutual funds that pay no dividends. If your children refrain from selling these securities until age fourteen or older, the IRS collects no kiddie tax, only adult long-term capital gains tax.

<u>Private Annuities</u>—You can open private annuities in your children's names, then fund these annuities by means of annual non-taxable gifts. You and your children pay no taxes on the gifts, and all future investment income inside the annuities grows tax-free until the withdrawal date.

<u>Life Insurance</u>—You can purchase a universal life insurance policy with one or more of your children as the owners and beneficiaries, then use annual non-taxable gifts to finance the premiums. All investment income inside the policy grows tax-free until the withdrawal date. If you feel uncomfortable about your children owning the policy, make the policy owner an Irrevocable Life Insurance Trust.

Spouse: The forgoing income shifting strategies usually offer no financial benefit for married couples. Why? Whereas children and their parents file separate tax returns, a husband and wife usually file a joint tax return. With a joint tax return, the couple's earnings will be added together to arrive at a single income figure, and taxed accordingly.

To avoid this negative tax treatment, a married couple might calculate their taxes according to both methods: married filing separately and married filing jointly. They can then decide which method best serves their financial goals.

Other Adults: The forgoing tax shifting strategies can be applied to your parents, relatives, and loved ones. Anyone you can trust with your money is a potential candidate for income shifting.

Shared Business Ownership: If you own a family business, you might consider this wonderful strategy. Structure your family business as a Family Limited Partnership ("FLP"), Limited Liability Company ("LLC"), or "C" or "Subchapter S" Corporation. A FLP and LLC offer the same liability protection as a corporation, and most of the tax advantages, for less costs, time, and trouble.

If carefully planned, a business entity can eventually shift 99% of your income to other family members. Why 99% instead of 100%? With only a 1% interest, you can still maintain 100% control of the business.

Here is how it works, using an FLP. First, you create the FLP, designating yourself as 1% general partner and 99% limited partner. Second, you place investment assets into the FLP.

Third, you invest and spend the assets as you alone decide. Finally, each year, in exchange for services or simply as tax-free gifts, you assign limited partnership interests to family members in lower tax brackets until they eventually own your 99% limited partner interest.

Your family now pays 99% of the business income taxes, but since they are only limited partners, they cannot control any part of the business. By retaining your 1% general partnership interest, you control 100% of the business, but you only pay 1% of the taxes.

In a nutshell, a properly structured family business enables you to enjoy assets tax-free for the remainder of your life, while your family pays taxes on those assets according to their lower tax rate. As an added bonus, your family will receive these assets free of estate taxes upon your death. Everyone wins, except the IRS, of course.

TAX STRATEGY #10

Shift Deductible Expenses to the Current Tax Year

This marvelous tax strategy involves shifting deductible expenses from a future tax year to the present tax year. When would you do this? When an income phaseout or deductible threshold would provide you more deductions in the current year. Why would you do this? To reduce your tax bite. You put the monetary difference between the two tax years into your pocket instead of into Uncle Sam's pocket.

Let's examine how business owners and ordinary individuals put this strategy into action.

Business Costs: As a business owner, during the final days of December, you might consider the purchase of equipment and supplies; the pre-payment of employee salaries, bonuses, and severance packages; next year's entertainment, marketing, and advertising expenses; prepaid trade journals, and association dues; and any charitable contributions.

Prepaid expenses that you cannot fully deduct in the current year include prepaid rent, insurance, and interest on loans. They must be deducted over the full contract or policy term.

Taxes: You should consider making payment of next year's property and income taxes on or before December 31st.

Mortgage: The IRS permits you to deduct one or more months of next year's mortgage payments in the current year, provided you mail a check to the lender by December 31st.

Investments: You can offset passive losses against passive gains resulting from the sale of securities and real estate. Just be careful about nonpassive gains derived from earnings, wages, and salaries. The IRS severely restricts the amount of passive losses that can be offset against nonpassive gains, although you can carryover any unused passive losses to future tax years.

Also watch out for "wash sales." You cannot take advantage of a passive loss from the sale of a security, unless you repurchase the same security more than thirty days after the sale.

Do you recall our tax shelter strategy concerning municipal bond swaps? This strategy best illustrates deduction shifting and wash sales. First, you purchase tax-free municipal bonds. If interest rates decreased in the current year, the value of your municipal bonds will normally increase. In such case, you defer any taxable gain by not selling the bonds. Alternatively, if interest rates increased in the current year, the value of your municipal bonds will normally decrease.

If and when your bonds decrease in value, you begin the "swap" by selling the devalued bonds in late December. After waiting at least thirty days to avoid a "wash sale," you purchase other equivalent municipal bonds in January or thereafter. In such case, you can deduct your passive bond loss against other passive gains in the current year.

Credit Cards: Here is an excellent opportunity to receive a deduction for expenses that you do not actually pay for during the current year. Purchases made with a credit card trigger a taxable event on the charge date, not the payment date. You can therefore charge and deduct an expense in the current year, even if you do not pay for the charge until the following year.

Deductible Deductions: Three big deductions come with a big "if" attached to them: deductions for medical bills, charitable contributions, and casualty losses. You can receive these deductions, but only if their amounts exceed a specific percentage of your adjusted gross income. To eliminate this obstacle, try bunching these deductions into a single year.

Gifts: Any annual gift in excess of a limited amount could subject you to gift taxes. With proper tax timing, you can double this gift limit. Instead of one gift, make two gifts: one on during the final week of December, and another during the first week of January. Each gift will constitute a separate tax year, provided the December check clears the bank on or before December 31st.

This completes the last three tax strategies that comprise our Holy Grail: maximizing the shifting of taxable income to future tax years and other taxpayers, as well as the shifting of deductions from future tax years to the present year. But don't stop reading just yet. I would like to share some final inspirational thoughts.

CHAPTER FIVE

▼

FINAL THOUGHTS

On February 3, 1913, our forefathers passed the Sixteenth Amendment of the United States Constitution, thus overruling an 1896 Supreme Court ruling that declared income taxes unconstitutional. This amendment declares:

"Congress shall have the power to lay and collect taxes on incomes, from whatever source derived, without apportionment among the several states, and without regard to any census or enumeration."

The passage of this constitutional amendment was made possible because most Americans believed in Robin Hood. You remember the story: rob from the rich and give to the poor.

At first everything worked just as planned. Congress only levied taxes on wealthy landowners. These taxes helped finance the federal government and provided assistance to the poor.

But soon thereafter, two events changed everything. On the one hand, our federal government quickly developed a ferocious appetite for money. It wasn't long before Congress needed to tax the middle class, and the poor, in order to satisfy it's insatiable hunger for tax dollars. In 1917, Americans paid eight hundred million dollars in taxes, $809,393,640 to be precise. By 1999, that figure nearly reached a mind boggling two trillion dollars, $1,917,642,000,000 to be precise. In less than a century, the federal government had expanded over 2,000 percent.

On the other hand, the rich got smarter. They hired the best tax attorneys and accountants to find every conceivable method of eliminating or substantially reducing their taxes, and they succeeded beyond their wildest dreams.

Meanwhile, the middle class and poor could not afford expert advice. As a result, the middle class simply continued paying their taxes without any relief. Since the poor had very little ability to pay taxes at all, and the rich had figured out how to eliminate or substantially reduce them, most of the tax burden fell upon the middle class. And that's where it remains to this day.

But now, regardless of your economic status, you can receive tax relief. By reading this book, you know exactly what the rich have known for decades. Every individual, whether rich, poor, or middle class, can reduce taxes. You no longer need to fear the IRS. They need to fear you.

Arise working class people of America. Reduce your taxes beginning today! You have nothing to loose but your chains, I mean your taxes. You have a world to win.

ABOUT THE AUTHOR

Biography

In 1976, Brent Jordan began his professional career in California as an Insurance Claims Adjuster, before becoming a licensed Private Investigator.

In 1987, Mr. Jordan became a member of the California State Bar, and practiced law in Los Angeles and San Francisco as a Trial and Appellate Lawyer. His San Francisco law firm eventually grew into four offices comprising five attorneys and thirty employees.

As a result of the untimely death of his law partner in 1994, Mr. Jordan developed a deep passion for estate planning. This life changing experience lead him to acquire a master of laws degree in Taxation (LL.M.).

In 2000, Mr. Jordan and his wife Kathy relocated to Las Vegas to raise their newly born twin sons Connor and Noah near their immediate family. Mr. Jordan then obtained Nevada State licenses as an Attorney, Life and Health Insurance Broker, Registered Securities Representative, and Notary Public.

Mr. Jordan is a member of the American, Nevada, California, and Clark County Bar Associations, the Southern Nevada Estate Planning Association, the Wealth Transfer Planning Network of Estate Attorneys, the Nevada Trial Lawyers Association, the Las Vegas Chamber of Commerce, the Channel 10 Planned Giving Committee, the Nevada Department of Life & Health Insurance, and the California Bureau of Private Investigators.

MISSION

Attorney Brent Jordan has a simple mission: to help you accumulate assets, protect them from economic predators, and pass them on to your family and loved ones for the least amount of costs, taxes, and time.

Every client shares one common goal: personalized service from a trustworthy professional for the lowest possible cost. Mr. Jordan has dedicated his career to making this goal a reality.

Your relationship with Mr. Jordan begins with a free consultation. At this first meeting, Mr. Jordan will answer your questions, review your financial portfolio, and present a customized plan that satisfies your personal goals. Mr. Jordan will then serve as your personal attorney and, if you desire, he will also become your Chief Financial Officer.

By obtaining State licenses as an attorney, registered securities representative, Life & Health Insurance broker, private investigator, and notary public, Mr. Jordan can handle all your financial needs, including IRS tax problems, tax elimination strategies, onshore and offshore asset protection, investment analysis, retirement annuities, life insurance, and estate planning.

But Mr. Jordan's interest in your financial security does not stop there. As a new client, you will be entitled Mr. Jordan's guaranteed "lowest fee" agreement, "free legal advice for life" program, financial seminars, and, most importantly, a no-charge periodical review of your entire financial portfolio by Mr. Jordan.

You may reach Mr. Jordan through his web site at **www.attorneyjordan.com**

0-595-21281-6

www.ingramcontent.com/pod-product-compliance
Lightning Source LLC
Chambersburg PA
CBHW031230280526
45784CB00004B/1511